A GOOD AND FAITHFUL SERVANT

A TRIBUTE TO DR. DVK SAMUEL
(20 APRIL 1953 – 24 APRIL 2021)

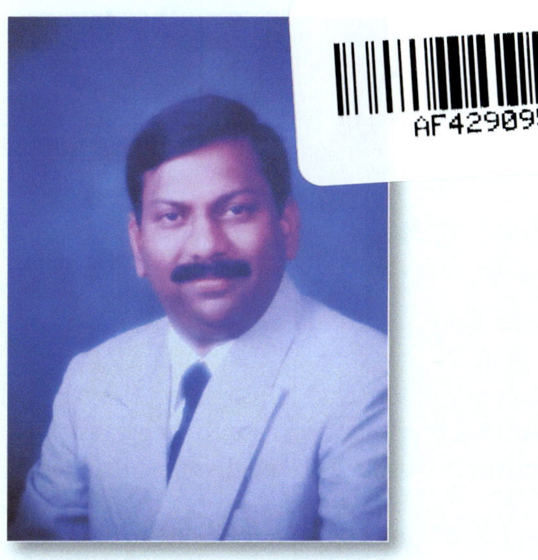

Alice Sarojini Samuel

"Then those who feared the LORD spoke to one another,

And the LORD listened and heard *them;*

So a book of remembrance was written before Him, for those who fear the LORD, And who meditate on His name."

Malachi 3: 16

Copyright © Alice Sarojini Samuel
All Rights Reserved.

With Wife and Children at Delhi

Dad

A dad is a person,
who is loving and kind,
and often he knows
what you have on your mind.

He's someone who listens,
suggests and defends.
Your dad can be one
of your very best friends.

He's proud of your triumphs,
but when things go wrong….
A dad can be patient,
helpful and strong.

In all that you do,
a dad's love plays a part.
There's always a place for you
deep in his heart.

And each year that passes,
we're ever too glad,
more grateful and proud
just to call him our dad.

Thank you, dad,
for listening and caring,
for giving and sharing.
But especially, for being just you.

We all miss you!

Come .....
Let's Walk down Memory Lane......

Foreword

I am grateful to God for a god-fearing father who was an epitome of patience, resilience and godly character. He loved the Lord tremendously and poured out his life in using the talents and gifts that God had given him for His glory and for the extension of God's kingdom.

As children, we were always very proud of our dad. He was a self-made man and would always give importance to education and hard work. He was a role model to us as he himself took every opportunity to further educate himself and work hard at improvising his skills and abilities.

He would always recite this Hindi doha to us while we would get too tired of studying. He would say "Atti ki ragad jo kare koi, agni prakat Chandan se hoye" which means that even though sandal wood is a cold wood if you work hard at it, it can produce fire. Similarly if you work hard at something and persist at it, you can achieve whatever you have set your mind at.

Dad was always meticulous and organised in his work. He would always make a check list for everything and made sure that every task or activity was planned in advance. He also made a plan for emergencies. I remember I had an extremely bad toothache when we were travelling in the train and dad had kept medicines in his purse for any such emergencies. Although Dad was a strong leader in his area of expertise, he was our papa at home. He was very loving and supportive and was strongly involved in bringing us up. I remember dad would always iron our school uniforms in the morning and give us warm clothes to wear in the winter mornings. He would help in feeding and bathing us when we were infants and would take us for cool evening walks after our dinner. We always enjoyed our evening walks because an ice cream vendor would stand at the far end of the road and dad would insist that it is now time to move back or he would say that he forgot to bring his purse with a slight naughty grin. We would play with dad and pull his hands or check his pockets and eventually dad would give in and we all would have a hearty laugh while choosing our icecreams.

During the last days, while he was battling the corona virus. He continued to trust in the Lord and knew that God was faithful. While we prayed without ceasing and trusted in the Lord, God gave us an assurance that "He would work all things for good to those who love him and are called according to His purpose and plan" (Romans 8:28). I want to thank my aunt and uncle for keeping their home and kitchen open during that time so that we could send hot, nutritious food to dad and Amit for taking care of mummy and being a strength to us as a family.

As a family we were completely broken and shattered after dad's passing away. Waves of grief still engulf us at times yet God has comforted and strengthened us as no one else could have. The verse from Isaiah 57: 1- 2 comes to my mind which says "The righteous perish and no one takes it to heart; the devout are taken away, and no one understands that the righteous are taken away to be spared from evil. Those who walk uprightly enter into peace; they find rest as they lie in death."

We have all been touched by my father's life and testimony. This book is dedicated to bring out the tributes paid by those who were close to him and admired his life in order to give God the glory and thank God for his beautiful life and legacy.

Mrs. Divya Jairaj
Daughter of Dr. DVK Samuel
Pune

Divya and Her Daughter, Naina

Dr. DVK Samuel - A Role Model

Dr. David Vijay Kumar Samuel, fondly called DVK was born on 20.04.1953 in Allahabad. He was the fourth son out of five boys born to Mrs. Virginia and Mr. Robert Samuel. He spent his childhood in Allahabad and did his schooling there and then went to Allahabad Agricultural Institute (AAI then) now called Sam Higginbottom University of Agriculture Technology and Sciences (SHUATS) to do his B Tech in Agricultural Engineering, soon after he did MTech from IIT K.G.P (1976-78), immediately after that he Joined ARS (Agri Research Services) in 1978 as Scientist. In the year 1981 he got married and in 1986 he went to IIT KGP to do his Ph.D. along with his family. He was a meritorious student all along and had received 3 scholarships for his studies.

Once he was back in Delhi, Dad was very active in various Christian organisations. Delhi Bible Fellowship the church we attended, he was appointed as a Deacon and was placed as a chairperson of the board for a set tenure. In Faith Academy the school we attended he was a member of the managing committee, chairman and was at times the acting manager. He played an active part in EU, EGF and UESI, CEF, Pusa Bible fellowship. He was a board member of Pandita Ramabai Mukti Mission, Bharat Seva Trust, Hyderabad and many such organisations. I remember also he was secretary of the Haggai Ministries Delhi Chapter.

He ministered to the students by having an open house. During our festivals, single people or students who could not go home were called over to have fellowship with us over a meal. Cell Group meetings were often held in our home which would always get concluded with a potluck dinner. As a child I remember going to Bengali market for lunch along with 3-4 families after attending church. We children took this opportunity to order what we liked. My dad wrote down everything and gave it to the waiter. There was no confusion at all, and we got what we wanted. His friends trusted him and looked up to him for advice many a times. He was simple, humble person. He had no airs about himself, always cool with no tension nor anxiety shown on his face.

He never came home saying don't, disturb me and was always available for us. He had published 70 papers written 3 books, some booklets and received 7 awards, developed or fabricated 23 machines, some of which were ready for commercial use and some patent applied for. Apart from Teaching M.Sc. Engineering students, he guided 12-14 students in their Ph.D. work. As a child I always wanted to study and work abroad, so when I finished my BTECH and was applying and appearing for competitive exams for MBA, my father asked me to appear for an interview for admission in MBA. I was thrilled to know I was selected and would be studying in UK. After completing my studies, I worked in the UK. In the Year 2008 I got married. I'm glad my father saw all his grandchildren and had wonderful conversations with them while playing along. He was Head of Post-Harvest technology centre for some time and then in the year 2015 he retired at the age of 62 as Head and Professor Division of Agricultural Engineering, IARI.

I thank God for my Father and it gives me great joy to say that my father has been a role model for me and my sister, he was indeed a leader who led by example and not by power or by controlling people. He was a very good listener and communicator, very logical in his thinking and encouraged people. A person who feared God (we had family prayers daily) and exhibited the fruit of the Spirit. His favourite song was "My Glory and the lifter of my Head". As a family we thank and praise God for his life. We are blessed to have had a father like him. The legacy he has left will surely be carried out by the grace of God. His Godly attitude, positive mindset and love will linger on in our hearts and push us to persevere to achieve our goals through Christ. On April 24th 2021 he went to be with the Lord and is enjoying in His presence, we miss you dad… until we meet again.

Your Loving Son and Daughter in Grace,

Amit and Renate Samuel

With Parents and Brothers

Receiving his Ph.D. Degree at Kharagpur in 1991

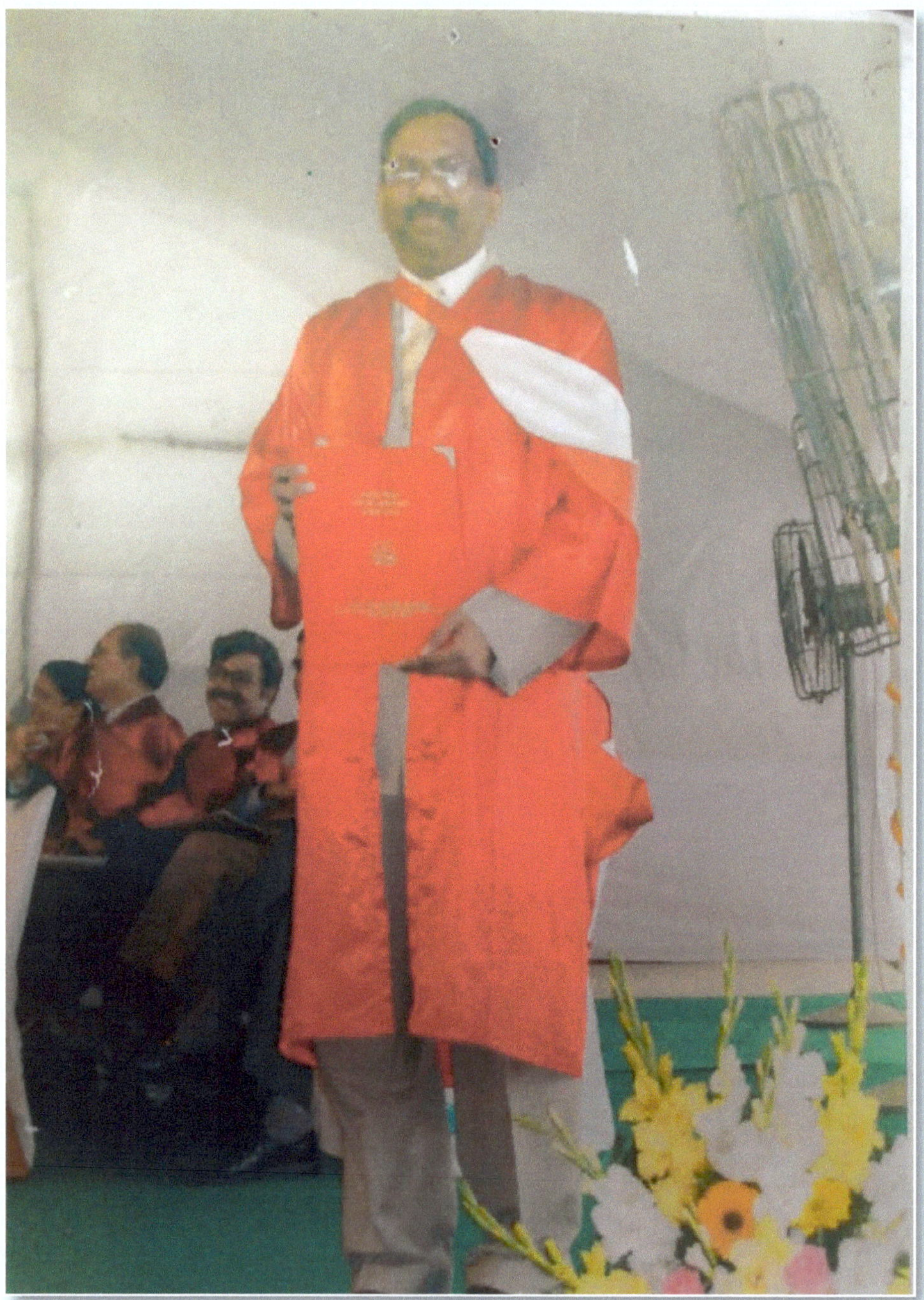

Best Teacher's Award- 2007

Visiting Professor- U.C Davis – U.S.A

At GCOWE, S. Korea 1995

Training at Haggai Institute 1994 Singapore

25th Wedding Anniversary

With Grandchildren: Kartavya, Kaelyn and Naina

Receiving Gold Medal for a Research Paper, 1995

Receiving Distinguished Services Certificate of ISAE, 2003

Dr. DVK Samuel, a Model Father, Husband and Servant of God.

We meet many people in our lifetime. Some we remember and some we don't. But some have influence on us for our lifetime because of the value system they practice. These values emanate from their commitment to the word of God and the desire to serve Him. Dr. DVK Samuel was one among them.

I met him in the early 90's when he joined the management of Faith Academy and had fellowship with him since then, till he was called home. The last time I talked with him was, on the phone when he was in the hospital admitted for Covid 19. When I said "I want to pray for you", he was very happy and said "Amen" at the end of our plea before God. Though he was battling with the dreaded disease, he kept his joy and faith in the Lord and Saviour Jesus Christ. And therefore, we know that he has gone to a much, much better place than here and those who have faith in Him will also reach His presence one day and we will see our brother there rejoicing in Him. Yes, the joy is for him and grief for us.

He was very prompt in attending all the meetings of Management and sub- committees of Faith Academy school and contributed immensely to various important decisions made particularly in the last one decade on various projects and schemes. He never hesitated to share his thoughts, though he knew that it may not be palatable to some at some time. He maintained his integrity to the cause of Christ, whether in his church or the school projects. His main contribution was that he got along with the committee members in all their decisions, though some time it might not have been his choice. What is important in a Christian fellowship is oneness and going together to face the challenges which he displayed throughout. An individual is important but fellowship and working together with others is more than that.

He was thoroughly a family man and loved his wife and children very dearly. As a responsible father he provided them whatever they needed in their life. Very jovial too at times. Whenever, we served Idly or Vada saying that it is good for the brain he will have a hearty laugh and enjoyed the joke and relished the food. It's my prayer that Alice and the children should know that the Lord has given, and the Lord has taken in His time and we must accept His will for DVK.

S. Robert
Director of Faith Academy Schools and projects

* * *

Being Recognized for His Services

As I know Sir .... Dr. DVK Samuel

Dr. DVK Samuel, an Agricultural Engineering Scientist and former Head of the Department from IARI, PUSA has been a member of Managing Committee of Faith Academy since 1992. I had a great privilege to know him in different capacities.

Great Personality:

One day as Principal, I introduced Sir to Faith Academy students in the beginning of a programme as an IIT Graduate, engineer, doctorate, professor, scientist and one of the resource persons of the green revolution in India. After the programme, Sir came to my room and said, "Please do not tell my titles. May all the glory go only to the Lord Jesus Christ." His humility made him a great personality!

Family values:

One day I asked Mrs. Alice Samuel, the former Head Mistress (primary) of Faith Academy how she could reach School every day before time. She answered me, "Sir, it is because of my husband. He helps me to prepare breakfast and packs up my bag with pen, pencil, eraser etc." What a great lesson for all of us!

Sir nourished his children in the fear of God. So later, they became not only big executives but also strong pillars of the church.

Scientific temper:

He used to judge students' science models patiently during science fair. Once a child gave an incorrect answer to his question. Still, he appreciated the child for her effort and explained the answer lovingly. The child felt very encouraged and motivated.

Linguistic skills:

Once a Hindi candidate was interviewed. His questions related to Hindi grammar were amazing. He also recited some Hindi dohas to our surprise. His Hindi was as excellent as his English.

Man of God:

Once, I went to attend a cottage prayer meeting in his house. The way he received the guests, students and the Lord's servants and gave his testimony was quite edifying. Our hearts were filled with the love of Lord Jesus Christ - His sacrifice on the Cross and resurrection. After the meeting was over, our stomachs were also filled with a sumptuous meal!

His contributions:

Dr. DVK Samuel retired as the Head of the Department of Agricultural Engineering, Pusa.

He had served Faith Academy in various capacities. During the years 1997-1999 and 2014-2016 he was the Honorary Chairman. He had also served sometimes as the Honorary Acting Manager. He was a member of the Building Committee and Convenor of Finance and Property Committee. His untiring participation and contribution to the construction of Phase III building of Faith Academy is commendable.

He also served Pandita Ramabai Mukti Mission.

May we thank the Lord Jesus Christ for his life and testimony.

Dr. M Kannan
(Principal of Faith Academy)

* * *

Dr. DVK as we used to call him was a person who enjoyed life. Our connection with the Samuels runs into more than two decades. As a board member he was there for all the meetings and our breakfast meetings were the best. He enjoyed the idli's, dosai and vadai and agreed with Mr. Robert that it is very good for the brains followed by his loud laugh which still lingers on.

The trips to Europe and Israel where Alice and DVK were inseparable and it was beautiful to see them together. He was a kind man and loved Alice a lot and every afternoon he will start calling if she has left school. A very affectionate person who was extremely fond of his children and grandchildren. It was very sad to hear about his home call but he is in a beautiful place where he will never grow old!!!

You will be missed!!!

Elizabeth Robert
Principal (Faith Academy - second shift)

* * *

A Tribute to David Samuel

*"Blessed is the man who does not walk in the counsel of the wicked
or stand in the way of sinners
or sit in the seat of the mockers. But his delight is in the law of the
Lord, and on his law, he meditates day and night.
He is like a tree planted by the streams of water,
yields its fruit in season and whose leaf does not wither.
Whatever he does prospers."* Psalm 1:1-3

To us, Dr. David Samuel's portrait is described well by King David in this Psalm. Being an agriculturalist David greatly appreciated the role of plants, trees and God's created world in our human existence. David' personal roots were deeply planted in the Life-giver – the Lord Jesus Christ. His nourishment for his daily existence was the Word of God – the Bible. This was clearly demonstrated in his love for the Word of God – whether it be in group Bible studies, hearing expositions of the scriptures in worship services, or in his home with his dear helpmeet Alice and his much-loved children. Just a few commendable observations that spoke of David's rooting in Jesus Christ: His concern for the spiritual welfare of many as he functioned as an elder and board member in Delhi Bible Fellowship; His reputation as a faculty member in the agricultural university (including his concern for the international students); His love and appreciation for his wife and children; His generosity towards the needy.

Though Brother David is no longer with us here on earth, his godly influence lives on in the lives of many of us. Though David is missed, we know with assurance that he is with the Lord Jesus in Glory.

Robert and Ruth Reid
Prince George, BC, Canada.

* * *

In addition to Beth's memorial of David Samuel below, I've added the following: As a novice in pastoral ministry, God encouraged me by sending some other men my age along with young couples with young children in love with God and seeking to be His faithful servants and followers. David Samuel a brilliant agricultural scientist from IARI Pusa joined our church, Delhi Bible Fellowship, along with his wife Alice and children Amit and Divya.

David and Alice became integral part of a core of passionate followers of Christ who served to integrate other families into DBF and together serve Christ as deacons, and later as elders and board members at DBF.

David also served Christ more widely in His body in EGF and as a long-standing board member, Vice Chair, and Chair at Faith Academy, New Delhi where his wife served as well-loved teacher and Headmistress.

David and Alice are dear friends of Beth and I and supported us in ministry with their prayers, encouragement, and godly advice. **Shalom!!**

Junias Venugopal
former Pastor Central Delhi Congregation
Delhi Bible Fellowship

* * *

To David: It is hard to believe it has been over a year since you have left us. I have so many good memories of my time with you. I came to India and lived from 1985 to 1993. As a foreigner and so far from my family and because we were in the pre-cell phone era, I was often homesick. This was always alleviated when I would have contact with you. Your gracious and warm spirit always made me feel so at home. I was inspired by what a wonderful and loving husband you were to Alice and father to Amit and Divya. You were such a support to Junias as he strived to grow the church.

You never were heavy handed with him but sought to encourage him with kind words and your gentle spirit. Not to mention your great ideas. Though you were accomplished professionally, you carried yourself with an air of humility and graciousness to all. David, I cannot imagine how much your wife, children and grandchildren miss you. I believe a part of you still lives on in them and you have shaped their lives in the best way possible. Thank you for all the ways you have made my journey in life easier and given me such a Christ-like example. You have left the world a better place and I thank God for letting me know you.

With love,

Your sister in Christ,

Beth Venugopal

* * *

I remember at our congregational member' meet, Dr. Samuel had some very encouraging words for a new church plant. This was very uplifting and precious for the pastoral team, who were labouring hard. This incident portrays his sensitivity and ability to uplift people.

At other instances, he had encouraged me, to continue serving with the hope we have in Christ. The encouragement from him, was rooted in the hope of the glorious future, which he would mention to me whenever we met.

And it is apt for me, to quote the future hope from, Philippians 3:20-21 "Our citizenship is in heaven and from it we await a Saviour the Lord Jesus Christ, who will transform our lowly body to be like His glorious body, by the power that enables Him even to subject all things to Himself."

Sqn Ldr Manav S Das
Lead Pastor (DBF central)

* * *

Dr. DVK Samuel, a man of all seasons Dr. DVK Samuel was a person par excellence. I first met him after my joining IARI, New Delhi in 1985. His positivity, enthusiasm, and plain-speaking endeared him to me. Our association for more than three decades gave us several opportunities to work together and it was always a pleasure working with him. Dr. Samuel was a very dependable professional colleague. He was a down-to-earth, soft spoken, ready to help, non-controversial, and a true professional. We always looked forward to his invitation to meet on New year to share greetings in person over the New Year Cake brought by him to the office. It is difficult to believe that Dr. Samuel has gone so far that we can meet him only in our thoughts.

Pitam Chandra
Former Director, ICAR-CIAE Bhopal, M.P

* * *

Our dear brother David, was a man after God's own heart. We remember him with very fond memories, a man who was always joyful, helpful, loving, kind and generous to his friends and family. He always took time with Alice every year to visit us in Delhi even with all the traffic inconveniences and their precious time taken. We miss him very much and what a glorious day it will be when we all meet our loved ones in our eternal home forevermore.

Ravi Richard
(Close friend)

* * *

I too have very, very fond memories of David, my brother whom we will miss now when we visit Delhi. Talking to me and my mother in Bengali. So sweet and caring and loving to all, especially to his family. A loving husband to Alice and a doting dad to his kids. Even though he was a scientist he had no airs about it. Truly a humble man of God and we will always cherish him and his sweet memories. You will always be in our hearts, David.

Mrs. Jharna Richard

* * *

David Samuel was a very intelligent person, he showed love to all his family members. He excelled in all aspects of life and finally he loved the Lord Jesus Christ.

Paul Prasad
(Alice's brother)

* * *

It was a pleasure to know Dr. DVK Samuel for a long time. We used to meet him in Delhi Bible Fellowship's common programmes. More than that, he was in the Child Evangelism Fellowship's committee for several years starting as a member and then he was the chairperson of the committee. He was very much committed to the Child Evangelism Fellowship's ministry, as he used to come regularly from a long distance, from PUSA campus, by his scooter to Gautam Nagar and go back late in the night. Dr. DVK Samuel was a gentle person in his dealings and in his talk. He always spoke in a soft voice and he never raised his voice. He also was a keen observer. Once while going through the financial statements in the Child Evangelism Fellowship's committee meeting, he asked how come there is income in the telephone column as there will be only expenses. That was the time we all had land line only. When we said, whenever we used the telephone for personal use, we put the money in income, he was both astonished and glad.

Praise God for his life used well for the Lord.

Prince and Seeli
Retired staff of Child Evangelism Fellowship

* * *

… "The one who showed him mercy."
Luke 10:37

After 9 months of my stay in Delhi where I started my life with a small job and after getting admitted in the most prestigious institute IARI to attain higher studies; I started feeling very lonely and was filled with many worries. I was unable to decide whether to continue with studies or leave this place and go back to my hometown, Vizag.

One afternoon, as I was still in a confused state, I happened to meet my HOD who with a smiling face had asked me whether I had lunch. I replied with a simple, 'Yes sir'. And he went on his way. But my vision followed his path and I felt that in a place where everyone is so busy, how come this man who is in such a big position noticed me and spoke to me.

I wanted to speak to him and share about my fears regarding my future so I went to his chamber knowing that he is a Christian from his name, at the same time keeping in mind that he is my HOD.

After gathering much courage, I spoke to him saying "Sir, what shall I do……. regarding my future and the problem, I am facing particularly to which church should I attend?"

He then answered me just as Jesus had replied to the man in **Luke: 10:25-37** and encouraged me of the Promise in **Jeremiah 29:11** that "God has plans to prosper you and not harm you and he has plans to give you hope and a future". Then he has introduced me to his family and church. Since then, sir and madam were my utmost support during my stay in Delhi. I received great help, care and love from sir. Every Sunday, he would call me and pick me from my hostel and take me to church. When I was low, he and his family would encourage me and show me God's love, they have been my greatest strength.

He was also a good teacher and had a childlike heart. He loved having ice-cream and panipuri with us students just as he would have with his own children.

He is a lovely host too. Birthdays were his favourite occasions to celebrate. Every year I saw him celebrate two birthdays with much love and enthusiasm; one, the birthday of his Creator: The Lord Jesus Christ and the other of his better half and love of his life, Alice Madam.

His friends, colleagues, neighbours and students were always on his list for Christmas. His way of celebrating Christmas was unique. His home was open to all with lots of food, a *special cake* made with his *own recipe, masala vada's* made by Alice ma'am, a cup of coffee, chocolates for kids and with a Gift for sure which was either a small booklet or calendar or simply through a greeting card with a promise of God on it. In this way he conveyed the gospel of love to the unreached.

He never forgot to celebrate madam's birthday and used to plan secretly surprising her each time.

From sir's life, I have learnt to be compassionate, loving and friendly and look unto 'My Glory and The Lifter of My Head' as he would sing very fondly. Today I have become a teacher and pray that I might be like sir who always loved everyone just as Jesus loved him. Inspired by his life, my husband and I have started following his way of celebrating Christmas with our fellow colleagues and friends who need to know the Saviour. As in **Proverbs: 10:7**, it is a blessing for us to remember him especially during Christmas.

He was **'A GOOD SAMARITAN'** who showed me God's path in a godly manner whom I shall always respect, follow, love and address as *'Samuel Sir'*.

Vimala, Bapatla,
Andhra Pradesh

* * *

I had known Bro. DVK Samuel for many years since our involvement in Haggai Institute. He had a passion for evangelism and teaching on evangelism. He had been a committed leader in the Church in Delhi especially in the Delhi Bible Fellowship where he was an elder. He and Alice loved the Word of God and were always ready to open their home for the Lord's ministry. I had the privilege of sharing the Word in their home on numerous occasions and was privileged to receive their warmth and hospitality. He is with the Lord Himself in Heaven and I pray for Alice and the rest of the family to move on and serve the Lord even more. I praise and thank God for the life and ministry of Bro. David Samuel.

Rajkumar Ramchandran
Logos

* * *

With Haggai Institute Members-Delhi

Dr. DVK Samuel was my brother-in-law, he was a very wise and intelligent person, he had made many innovations in his department, he was called by reputed institutions one being CFTRI (Central Food Technological Research Institute) in Mysore, Karnataka for consultations, seminars etc. He was very active in his church. He was a good father to his children and a loving husband to my sister, Alice.

May God Bless his generations to come.

Samuel Prasad and Family
(Alice's brother)

* * *

We had the privilege of growing up with David, watching him grow up to be a highly generous man with a big heart. He was a well behaved and loving individual. I have the best childhood memories of him. God bless his family 🙏

Daniel Dixon
(David's cousin)

* * *

It was with deep shock and profound sadness that we heard the passing of our much loved and highly esteemed neighbour, (Satyam Member & Owner of Flat no B -101, Satyam Society). Dr. DVK Samuel (Former HOD (Engg division), Pusa Agriculture University), after contracting coronavirus and pneumonia. He was hospitalized at Hubli, Karnataka and left for his heavenly abode on 24th April 2021 leaving behind his wife, two children and 3 grandchildren. Dr. DVK Samuel won the respect of his colleagues because he combined kindness with sheer talent. He is someone with strong faith, wisdom and humour. He was fiercely dedicated to his family and loved them with all his heart. He always told us to be strong, and to continue to love and believe in God. One could trust in what he would say. He was always looking to make people happy. He was passionate about helping others who were less fortunate and always had a smile on his face, a laugh in his heart and a tune on his lips. He was involved with other local, national and international organizations that helped people in need. After the painful loss, it is easy to imagine ways it could have been avoided. Adding to the emotional hardship of losing a loved one to coronavirus is the cessation of traditional rituals such as memorials and funeral services that help relatives say goodbye. May God console and comfort sister Alice, Amit and Divya as well as the grandchildren.

K. A Issac
(Co-resident at Satyam Apartments, New Delhi)

* * *

My grandfather is the best man I have ever known. He treated me like a princess. On his death bed he told he wanted to see his grandchildren. I feel his presence with me all the time and even when I am sad. I miss him a lot and I love him very much.

Kaelyn
(DVK's granddaughter)

* * *

My grandfather as I lovingly called him "Nana", was a sweet and kind man. He was very funny and loved to crack jokes with us. He was also fond of travelling and took me to various places like Nainital, Mussoorie and Ooty. He loved to eat Chinese food and both of us loved eating ice- cream. He was very intelligent and bright. I miss you a lot!!

Naina
(Granddaughter of Dr. DVK Samuel)

* * *

Uncle David, as we fondly called him, was a gentleman in character and always forthcoming to anyone who approached him. He was warm and always cracked jokes when we were around him. He often shared from his life experiences on family, job and other life matters through biblical principles which he had acquired and lived over the years. He loved his family and it was evident in the way he loved his children and others. Thanking God for giving us the opportunity to meet and know Uncle, Alice Aunty and their family. God bless you all abundantly.

Vaidhy, Sarah & Ashira
(One church- Pune)

* * *

As God's household in Pune, we knew uncle and family for the last three year of his earthly journey. A straightforward, punctual and methodical person with a barrage of experience in his professional front and Service to God's Kingdom. So much to learn in all his conversation especially about his passion in serving our Lord and Saviour Jesus Christ. One such experience that he shared was his visit to the FMPB mission field in Gujarat, a tribal village where the local people encounter all sorts of wildlife, he was courageous enough to stay in a tent in the middle of the forest with the missionaries and minister to the local people. Truly we miss all his real-life stories which are so encouraging. We as a family are so glad to know David Uncle's family.

Praveen, Ann, Joshua and Nathan
(One Church Pune)

* * *

I first met Dr. David Samuel when I moved to Delhi in 2001 with my work for The Leprosy Mission.

I joined the worship at Delhi Bible Fellowship, which was where David and Alice Samuel and their children, Amit and Divya also worshipped. They made me very welcome and we became very good friends.

They lived at the Indian Agricultural Research Institute where David was a Professor and Head of his Division, and I lived in Inderpuri, adjacent to IARI.

I joined their Bible Study Home Group and they often invited me to their home. I remember especially our times at Christmas, when they would invite me after Church on Christmas morning. We would go back to their home for Christmas dinner and spend the time making Christmas "goodies" for David's non-Christian colleagues from The Agricultural Institute whom they had invited for tea, using the opportunity for Christian witness.

I also remember very well my 60th birthday in 2008, (and retirement, so I would soon be returning to the UK). They invited me to their home in the evening and we went out for a lovely meal along with a Birthday Cake for me.

After I returned to UK, I was so pleased that they were able to come and stay with me in my home at Suffolk in 2010 and we had a lovely day visiting Colchester together.

David was also most helpful to me by liaising with the Inderpuri SBI regarding my bank account there, after I had returned to UK.

David was so very kind and a good advisor to me. But most of all he loved the Lord Jesus and was a brother in Christ. I was very sad to hear of his demise, but we know he is now in glory with the Saviour whom he loved and served and we will meet again.

Margaret Mahato
Capel St Mary, Ipswich, Suffolk, UK
Previously with The Leprosy Mission in India.

* * *

Prof. Dr. Sh. DVK Samuel (Late)

DVK Samuel uncle and Alice aunty in the very first meeting itself, you guys became so close to our heart. It is very rare that we get to meet people like you, in our entire life time. I have heard and met people prophesying Christ, but hardly saw a few who live like Christ and you were one in whom I saw Christ living. It is very unfortunate that we got so less time to meet, talk and share, you have left a great mark on our lives. Uncle, your down to earth, striking personality, stylish & fast driving at 60s, graceful & affectionate talk took us by storm every time we met.

We miss you a lot uncle….! & We hope to meet you soon in Christ!!

With lots of love and regards!!!

Sushma & Arun Kumar
Mrs. Sushma B, Assistant-I,
Indian National Science Academy, New Delhi

* * *

Dr. DVK Samuel- A Colleague's Few Remembrances

Sometimes it is difficult to choose appropriate words to describe a friend with whom one has had deep and long association. I have the same sentiments. When I shifted to IARI from CRRI, Cuttack, I had fortune to get timely help. Although IARI was no new place for me since I had studied there but that was long time ago, a logistic support was very essential. Since I had not met him before, I was deeply impressed by this ever smiling and helpful colleague.

Dr. Samuel, who had come from NDRI, Karnal before me, was a very knowledgeable person with whom it was a great pleasure to interact on various themes, most often in areas of common interest since we had same specialisation. There is a special advantage of IARI that it offered PG Courses and those of us who loved teaching and research guidance, it provided welcome opportunity. So, we formed a good Team for giving boost to research and teaching in post-harvest engineering and technology. We took the courses together. Dr. Samuel was much liked by his colleagues in the Division of Agricultural Engineering and students due to his very endearing and helpful nature. Later, I took over as Head of Division in which position, I remained for two terms. This period was utilised for creation of new and expansion of existing labs, refurbishing workshop and construction of greenhouses. In this endeavour, Dr. Samuel's contribution was significant. Interestingly, we never had any difference of opinion since we saw the same dreams for expansion of the Division and profession. Since during this period, I had also held responsibility in the Indian Society of Agricultural Engineering and Bi-monthly Publication Agricultural Engineering Today, I often sought help from Dr. Samuel which he was glad to provide.

One more thing which I would like to mention that since he came from Allahabad, he spoke in chaste Hindi which many of us enjoyed. I used to ask him about his command of Hindi, he would tell that he loved this Language. Of course, his English was also impeccable which came out through his interactions and lectures.

Initially we used to stay in the Kaveri Apartments, this gave opportunity to our families to socialise. Later on, we moved to other premises. After some time, I took an assignment with Afro-Asian Rural Development Organization and served there for four years and returned to Division for a very short period before being asked by ICAR to join a position at Krishi Bhavan. After that I never came back to Division. So, our interactions became a few and far between. But I used to be in touch especially since he took over as Head of Division. When I retired and settled in Delhi, he would often request me to take some classes. It was so nice of him, but I could not avail the opportunity.

Dr. Samuel will always be fondly remembered as a dear friend and colleague.

Dr. Syed Ilyas

* * *

My Gratitude to Bro DVK Samuel

I have very pleasant memories of dear brother DVK Samuel or DVK as we would call him during my days with DBF from 2002 onwards. As I remember him in the first anniversary, 3 things come to my mind.

1. **Humility:** Even though Bro DVK held a very important position at the PUSA institute, he would mingle with everyone, including the budding youth at the same level.

2. **Positive Attitude:** I cannot forget his ever-smiling face and the positive attitude with which he would address even difficult issues at church and in the Men's fellowship.

3. **Encourager:** Bro DVK was a great pillar of strength and had a wonderful source of courage for all who needed counsel and guidance. He had an amazing way to lift the spirits of the people who were down with their own challenges and bring them back to their feet to move onward, not only in their faith in Christ but also in their daily lives.

Anand Pillai
MD, Leadership Matters Inc.

* * *

In Memory of Dr. DVK Samuel

A thorough gentlemen and a godly soul committed to church and its mission

I first met Dr. DVK Samuel in 1995 in evening worship of Faith Church at Faith Academy. He was an unassuming, ever smiling, easy to talk to person. I had just graduated and was appointed to assist the main pastor at Faith church. The evening service constituted of very educated and well-placed people. Dr. Samuel himself was a notable professor of engineering in the department of Agriculture engineering (later he went on to head the same) at the famous Pusa institute (Indian Agriculture Research Institute). In the beginning I was scared to pastor such a group and felt very nervous. Dr. Samuel was one among those who helped me and encouraged me.

Dr. Samuel and his family later became a source of encouragement as family for me, my wife and our two kids. We often visited them and fellowshipped with them.

In 2000 at Faith Church, we took a challenging step of starting mission work in different areas of Delhi, although we were a small congregation. With our senior pastor John L. Dorsey, we coined a phrase "let us get our feet wet" from the book of Joshua. Dr. Samuel was among the first one not only to encourage us but also to contribute to it. He was equally committed in his works as in his words.

He is now with his Savior, enjoying the joy and warmth of his love. We miss him among ourselves for great Christian fellowship and encouragement. He is ever remembered in our family and we are eternally indebted to his contribution in our lives.

Rev. Hiralal Solanki
Associate Pastoral Co-Ordinator
Indian Reformed Fellowship – Australia

* * *

It was August Sunday morning in 2011, I had found DBF, a church near Gole Market, convenient to reach by Metro, since I had no vehicle then. Longing for fellowship, I was introduced to Pastor Jeremy Dawson, over a cup of coffee, where I had made known my desire. He found Dr. David Samuel, who told about the cell group meeting at his residence. For the first time, I was introduced to Dr. David and his wife Mrs. Alice. As they were happy to have me over for their mid-week Bible study on Wednesday, they shared their residential address of Pusa Campus of Agricultural college and Dr. David's phone number. Next Wednesday evening, I ventured out on a cycle rickshaw, after contacting Dr. David over phone. With my broken Hindi, I was struggling with the rickshaw puller. To my utter surprise, Dr. David was eagerly waiting on the road side for me, then I realised his HUMILITY to come down and wait for me, a new visitor. After 2 months stay in this big city, I had found warmth of fellowship of a family as Mrs. Alice welcomed me with a hot cup of tea. That was the beginning of our Association with their family which grew stronger after my wife, Shaila arrived from Mumbai in May 2012. We as a couple, got introduced to Mrs. and Dr. David Samuel, the friendship further grew as Shaila got employed in Faith Academy, where Mrs. Alice was Headmistress. Whenever a special speaker visited their house, brother David always informed me in advance so that I could plan my evenings to be part of the assembly. When I purchased the car, I took it to his residence and he appreciated my choice of Honda Amaze, though he had a much bigger car, Toyota Etios. Dr. David introduced us to many of his Christian friends, like Mr. John Samuel's family, Mrs. & Mr. Kothapalli's and Dr. and Dr. Mrs. Shenoy. In 2014, as there were series of holidays, both (we both) and David's family members decided to visit Nainital, but our stay could be arranged only in Sat Tal. It was quite an adventurous trip, with a boat ride and visits to places of wonderful scenic beauty. We learnt some basic cooking to keep ourselves fed. In the meantime, we got introduced to their children, Amit and Divya and their family members; as Divya and her daughter had accompanied us to Nainital. We also enjoyed easter morning services with Mrs. and Dr. David who took us to Lodhi Gardens with other Christian friends; those services were new and refreshing to us. Later, I received my transfer order to Bangalore. After we packed and sent our household goods, there were still 5 hours to take our flight. Then I received a call from David informing us that they would visit us to bid final goodbye from Delhi. In the evening, both Mrs. and Dr. David brought us refreshments and tea to feed us and take care of us. After my retirement, when we shifted to Hubli, both Mrs. and Dr. David, visited us at Hubli as their son also stayed there. The close brotherhood and camaraderie grew and brought us even closer as they shifted to Pune to be close to their daughter. But his next visit to Hubli in 2021 was devastating as he was brought as a Covid patient, which turned out to be tragic and fatal as he left us to his heavenly abode. Because of Covid restrictions we could not be present at his funeral which aches me even today. Hope to see you brother David in the presence of Jesus.

Mr. L. Birnur
(Retired bank manager)

* * *

Brother David's encouraging words were like a brother born for adversity. We always looked up to him when our faith was shaken. His life proved that he was a true legend. We are at a loss on earth. I cannot find words to describe how I miss him.

Mrs. Shantini John

* * *

My Memories of Loving Brother Dr. DVK Samuel

It was the year 1987 and the month of July, when I joined the Indian Institute of Technology at Kharagpur (IIT-KGP) as a student. There I met Dr. DVK Samuel (fondly and respectfully referred as "Samuel Bhaiya") for the first time. The Christian Fellowship at IIT-KGP was meeting at his home at the Zakir Husain Hall of Residence. There were very few Christians studying or working there at that point in time, and we (Ramachandran, Johnson, Jithendran and myself) all longed to meet this loving family - Samuel Bhaiya, Alice didi and their lovely little children - Amit & Divya. Bhaiya and didi were very much welcoming and spent considerable amount of their time besides also sharing meals with us. As an example, I quote as Jithendran (Jit) recalls the experience of visiting their home for Bible studies as a refreshing experience for him. He being a new Christian then recollects this as the only dose of familial comfort and warmth that he experienced amidst the otherwise dreary week. This experience had a huge impact in our lives. Bhaiya was the one who introduced me to the local Baptist Church there in Kharagpur, where I continued for several years during my stay there.

After completion of his Doctoral Program at IIT-KGP, Bhaiya worked for several years at the Indian Agricultural Research Institute (IARI) at Pusa, New Delhi and was staying at IARI Staff Quarters. I had visited them there as well and he took me to the Delhi Bible Fellowship where he was also a spiritual leader in that church. Thereafter we could not meet face to face, but did have good conversations over phone with Bhaiya. He still had the same warmth, I used to feel earlier talking to him.

During all these interactions, I observed Samuel Bhaiya to be a very kind and loving person. He accepted us as we are, and was non-judgemental; as a result, we used to feel extremely comfortable and well encouraged talking to him. He always had time and space for people. He deeply cared for us, our families, our profession our spiritual life and thus for our overall wellbeing. He was very mindful of the different members of our fellowship. With a keen interest he enquired about each one of them whenever we connected. He was passionately following Christ and had a special interest and God given skills on several areas including Christian administration, mentoring, encouraging to name a few. Bhaiya served the purpose of God in his generation, in the place and circumstances where he was placed, bringing glory to the God who saved him! Praise be to God!

Rajkumar Gell

* * *

Dr. DVK Samuel was introduced to Mukti Mission by Mr. Paul Samuel in the 90's to bring his vast experience into the Mukti farm and Education. The hours spent in restructuring some of the issues in terms of salary increase to the staff, to provide for residents something different was in his heart. The strict compliance to core values of Mukti was much appreciated. The Mukti family fondly remembers his contribution to the overall development of ministry of Mukti Mission which cannot be overstated. Contributing personal resources and putting a word of encouragement to the staff and residents as part of Pastoral Care is something which we are grateful for.

Anil Francis
Chief of operations. Pandita Ramabai Mukti Mission

* * *

"Dr. Samuel was one of the greatest characters of academic and scientific fraternity" His passion to serve the poor, needy and marginalised section of society and approachability to all made him different than others. He was loved by all in Pusa campus and across the ICAR system. I have several memories instilled within me………. but unable to pen down. You are still around us; we can feel and celebrate your thought and act in our daily life. You are alive forever as your words of wisdom will keep on spreading by your students and fellow colleagues."

Dr. Ram Asrey, Usha Yadav, Aayush & Anwesha
15-C Scientist Apartment, IARI, Pusa campus, New Delhi-110012

Tribute to Brother DVK

It is my privilege and honour to write a tribute to Dr. DVK Samuel, or Brother DVK as we called him. I knew him for 20+ years. As an agricultural scientist, he visited the World Vision India project site at Nainital, Uttarakhand, and provided technical support around post-harvest technology in the year 1999. Based on his advice we were able to set up farmers associations and cold storages. As a family, we had wonderful times of fellowship with Brother DVK as part of Central Delhi EGF. He was excellent in teaching the Word and passionate in reaching out to students for the Lord. His home was a home away from home for many students. His camaraderie with children, including our children, was a delight to watch.

He was also an active member of the Delhi Bible Fellowship and provided leadership as an elder in the Central Delhi Congregation and served on the DBF Board. DBF has been tremendously blessed by his excellent leadership.

He was like an elder brother to me and I cherish the times we spent in conversation.

May God comfort and shower His kindness to the bereaving family.

K.A. Jayakumar
Director - Strategic Alliances, World Vision India, New Delhi

* * *

Samuel, my dearest

A friend taken from life too soon is nothing but tragedy. His death affects everyone who knew and loved him and they will always honor his legacy and remember him. This quote is attributed to my Dearest and closest friend cum former colleague Dr. David Vijay Kumar Samuel whom I first met in 1976 after his entry at Indian Institute of Technology (IIT), Kharagpur, West Bengal for pursuing post graduate studies. I was senior to him by one year in the same course in the same institute. Though we served different ICAR institutes as Scientist S-1 during our initial professional career since 1978, we joined Indian Agricultural Research Institute (IARI), New Delhi as Scientist S-2 in 1983 within a gap of about one month. Being a senior person considering joining time, he helped me a lot to complete all official formalities after joining. We together joined IIT, Kharagpur on the same date in 1986 to pursue Ph. D. and rejoined IARI, New Delhi after expiry of our study leave period of 2 years. Since then, till 1997 we were together at Div. of Agril. Engg., IARI, New Delhi sitting together in the same room and acting as associates in the research projects before I left Delhi to join National Instt. Of Natural Fibre Engineering and Technology (NINFET) earlier known as National Instt. of Research on Jute and Allied Fiber Technology (NIRJAFT) at Kolkata in Jan. 1998 as Principal Scientist. Even then we had regular contacts and frequent mutual visits to residence along with family. A number of times, our families together visited tourist places outside Delhi and attended religious and other festivals at home irrespective of caste a and community we belong to. However, after retirement from service, our interaction reduced gradually with passage of time and I was taken aback after receiving the shocking message from Mrs. Samuel of his untimely and sudden death after a long and protracted illness. He always had a big smile and a terrific sense of humor. The bond between us is beyond the mortal world.

A best friend gone too soon is a tragedy. But what would have been worse is never to have met him. I am grateful to have been David's friend in life and will continue to be his friend in death, honoring him in all I do. Grief is often different when a friend passes away due to illness or accident. A true friend is never truly gone. Their spirit lives on in the memories of those who loved them. Warmth is found through fond memories. There is no greater memory than the sound of his laugh. Let me grieve for the bond we shared and the bonds we didn't get a chance to form yet. Friendships formed in life are broken in death but the love we shared remains unbreakable.

Dr. Debasis Nag
Former Director, ICAR-NINFET
Kolkata

* * *

I am very delighted to say a few words of my close association with Dr. DVK Samuel since I met him in 1992 in DBF Triveni Congregation. I was teaching in Grace Bible College with the responsibility of the Registrar of the college. But in the weekends, I used to come to my newly bought Apartment in Paschim Vihar (West Delhi) to conduct a Bible study group on Saturday night and worshipped at DBF Triveni Congregation and returned to Grace Bible College. My intention was to plant a church in Paschim Vihar. Dr. DVK was one of the deacons at Triveni Congregation and the then Pastor Rev. Junias Venugopal delegated him to interview me for DBF membership. This was when I became closer to him. I shared with him, my vision to plant a church in Paschim Vihar and he was full of joy, encouraged me to plant it as a DBF congregation. He then introduced me to Pastor Junias and shared with him my vision of planting a church in West Delhi. I found in DVK a good friend, a big brother and a humble Christian leader. In short, we continued that relationship all through my life and ministry in and around DBF, and even after my family relocated to Australia. I had the privilege of serving God with him in his various capacities, as the DBF Board Member, Treasurer, Chairman, Mission Committee Member, Property committee Chairman etc. He was one of the humblest brothers I had have ever met and have had such long association and friendship with him. The last time I met him physically was at the DBF 50th year Anniversary celebration and this is what he said to me as he hugged me, "You are my favourite Pastor." I know I don't deserve it, but I took it as an honour for the glory of God. I truly lost a good friend and a big brother.

My prayers are with Alice Samuel specially and their children Divya and Amit. God bless you all.

Rev. Dr. Thayil John
Pastor, Keiraville International Church
Wollongong, Australia

* * *

A Eulogy for Dr. David Samuel

The heart fills with joy at the thought of a warm, jovial, kind and ever-smiling person but soon has to contend with sadness upon being faced with the prospect of life without the physical presence of such a person. My family and I lived right opposite the Samuels in Kaveri Apartments, Pusa, during the late 80s and early 90s. Our children were friends with each other and spent all day barging in and out of each other's tiny flats and playing and running up and down the corridors. Our elder daughter, Rachita, was childhood friends with Amit and Divya. With the arrival of our younger daughter, Arpita, in 1992, the three musketeers became four. Our families were close and we celebrated all the major festivals, like Diwali, Holi and Christmas, together. Alice, a fellow Kannadiga, added to the close ties we all enjoyed. Even though we moved into a new accommodation in the mid-90s, we kept in touch and continued to visit each other—Christmastime is especially vivid in my memories, thanks to the wonderful memories of all the good times and goodies Alice and David presented to us. Dr. Samuel was well respected and was held in high esteem by all his colleagues. His simplicity, kindness, happy demeanour and helpful nature endeared us throughout and will be remembered for long. With such noble qualities, David no doubt would have found pride of place at the altar of God and in the Kingdom of Heaven.

Dr. N.T Yaduraj
*Formerly Director,
ICAR- Directorate of Weed Research, Jabalpur
National Coordinator,
National Agricultural Innovation Project (ICAR) and
Principal Scientist ICT4D, ICRISAT, Hyderabad*

* * *

Dr. DVK Samuel's part of life's journey started in the year 1976 at Indian Institute of Technology Kharagpur. I was an occasional visitor to Union Baptist Church, Kharagpur. I had the opportunity of meeting Dr. Samuel at Church along with other IIT ian's, who also attended Union Baptist Church. I had come out of IIT in the year 1977and got a job near Delhi. In the meantime, DVK got to know the Prasad's family though Alice was staying with her grandmother and studying in a college near Bangalore. During the demise of Alice's mother in Karnataka in the month of March 1978. He took the challenging role of taking care of the siblings as Alice's father flew immediately to Karnataka. Daily DVK would take Sam (Alice's brother) to appear for his class XII board exams.

It was in the year 1980 that I got married to Alice's elder sister and he too decided to settle down soon with his fiancé Alice. It was then in 1981 that I got close to them.

From then on it was a prosperous journey of DVK and Alice.

He was very hard working, always ready to take up challenges in his career. He helped innumerable people with whom he came across. He was a fun-loving person always looking forward to enjoying the holidays with his family. We used to combine our holiday trips together and visited various places. He was associated with various Christian organisations and worked voluntarily in various capacities with the desire to improve the conditions of the poor and needy. In his professional career he had done various researches, written several papers, patented machines in the Agricultural field.

After his retirement he kept himself busy with children, grandchildren and other Christian organisations.

He ended his golden life's journey on 24 April 2021.

We all miss our dear Dr. DVK SAMUEL. May God bless all his works, his family members and his associates.

Prabhat and Mary
Canada

* * *

It was my privilege and honour to have come to know brother David Samuel during his lifetime. He was a highly accomplished man throughout his life, from his higher studies to his professional career. Despite these laudable achievements, he was one of the most humble and approachable people I have come across. His level of involvement in the life of the church is a testament to his commitment to the family of God. As I reminisce on my interactions with him, I am reminded of his sense of humour that always helped me appreciate the lighter side of life. His joy that flowed out of his deep faith in God was infectious. He will be deeply missed because it is impossible to fill his space in the corporate life of the church. We bid him farewell with the hope of the resurrection that we have in Christ. It is only for a little while that we part ways till, we meet again at Jesus' feet.

Mathai Samuel

* * *

Mr. DVK Samuel was a long-standing member of the DBF family and has served in various important roles over the years. He was a passionate lover of the word of God and was very encouraging to the young people. He would love to have conversations with them after the services. He would have something nice to say about the music or the sermon. He was always a friendly and approachable person on Sundays.

Just a short while before he left Delhi, I was appointed as the lead pastor. He always had kind and encouraging words to share with me. He would even compliment my choices of tie to go with my suit on some Sundays and dared me to be adventurous in my choice of tie. He told me one day he would take me tie shopping to get some really cool ties. I enjoyed our conversations whether light hearted or deep and theological. And I know that is not just my experience. You would always find him surrounded by people. He knew how to be deep and serious and yet he knew how to have a good laugh. He will be missed and remembered with much love and gratitude.

Sandeep Christian

* * *

The memory of the righteous is blessed. Proverbs 10:7

I am Laura Elizabeth, cousin of Alice and sister-in-law of DVK, living in Mumbai, Kalyan.

On this solemn occasion my memories take me way back to the period of 1900's. My parents late Rev. D. Rajarathnam and Padmini, also my paternal uncle late L. Prasad and maternal aunt Rawamani (Alice's parents).

Very often our family used to go to Kharagpur during our vacation. Uncle's children Sam to Tabitha and my children Johnny, Gracy and Jacob used to have good fun, they were full of mischief playing together. They enjoyed sightseeing in Calcutta.

God had also given us the privilege of attending all the sibling's marriages except Sam and even some of their children. I had the opportunity to attend the nuptials of both Amit's and Divya's.

Our association with DVK was after his marriage to Alice. He was a thorough gentleman. His nature was full of love, kindness, concern and hospitality. He was a God-fearing man involved in Christian meetings, conferences and charitable events. Our last get together was at Hubli during Joshua's wedding. Those sweet memories are still fresh in our minds.

May God grant peace, comfort and solace to his family and also to his extended families.

Let us all hope and live with faith that one day we would meet him in Heaven, the new kingdom of our Lord and Saviour Jesus Christ!

May God bless you all! Amen

Laurakka and Devadanam
Mumbai

* * *

Memories of Dr. DVK Samuel

Whenever, I think of the days in the Managing Committee of Faith Academy, I cannot forget Dr. DVK Samuel who was always remembered as DVK. In the meetings we sat mostly next to each other as his love for me was special. After the meetings, we used to share about our children's studies & their future. I learnt many blessed things from DVK. He was very regular to all the meetings when he was not out of station or abroad. He was very good & instantaneous in his prayers in the meetings & other gatherings of members & staff. He had no jealousy or hatred against any member or staff of FA. Mostly I recorded the minutes of MC meetings, & if any minute was not properly worded, he used to gently point out before correction. DVK was very friendly with everyone whether Principal, HM, Staff or even peon. If any staff had a problem or difficulty, DVK used to listen to them patiently before taking such grievances to the Principal or Manager. With him, I personally enjoyed every meeting or gathering.

I always respected his qualifications & his special interest in guiding his Ph.D. students. DVK loved to take his family to all possible places in India as well as abroad. His reverence for God & his fear of God is admirable. I am very proud for having such a wonderful friend through Faith Academy. May God bless all his children & grandchildren to carry forward DVK's legacy to future generations.

C.E.M. Dhinakaran
Former member of MC& CES of Faith Academy.

* * *

With Students at Pusa Bible Study

With MC Members- Faith Academy

Dr. DVK Samuel a Close Family Friend

I thank God for the life of Dr. DVK Samuel, a very close family friend of ours. We were neighbours in IARI New Delhi for many years. Our children grew up together in the same campus. We have many wonderful memories of our dear brother. A fine believer of the Lord Jesus Christ and he had shared the love of Christ with many students and colleagues at IARI and other places where he worked. His house was always open for God's ministry, prayers and Bible studies. He was deeply involved in Church activities. He was an active member of the Pusa Bible study group where Rev. John L. Dorsey used to teach the Bible to the students and some Scientists. He was one of the organizers for the Christmas Programme arranged for Pusa students, Scientists and other friends every year. He had a close relationship with my husband Dr. AVN Paul. Both of them were associated with Faith Academy also for a long time. Whenever they met, they used to share many things with each other. Brother was a friendly person, cheerful and encouraging. Whenever we faced difficulties in life Dr. DVK Samuel stood with us and supported us.

He was a great scientist whenever I took Faith Academy students for educational trips to his lab, museum and workshop where different kinds of farm implements were displayed, he personally greeted the children and explained the uses and demonstrated the working of the different tools and machines with lots of patience and passion. Children enjoyed their visits. He was always ready to help anyone in need. Once around midnight my son fell down from the bunk bed and his head hit the edge of a table. There was a deep cut and he was bleeding profusely. I went to their house and knocked on the door. Brother came immediately and gave first aid to my son.

He loved all the members of sister Alice's family. He opened his house and gave all the support required when his Sister-in-law Tabitha was undergoing treatment. Samuels were known for their hospitality. Both of them loved the people around them. On Christmas Day they received many guests and were busy serving all homemade goodies. Their home-made Christmas cake and kababs were very popular among the friend's circle. They were yummy because brother used to select the ingredients with so much care and knew the correct proportion in which they should be added. He loved his family very much. He was a loving father to Amit and Divya. Divya was his darling daughter. Sister and brother always used to go to all the places together. It was a joy to see them at weddings, church functions and during other celebrations. We miss him. He is happy in God's presence. We will always cherish the wonderful memories we have. Praying for God's blessings on sister Alice, children and grandchildren.

Nirmala Paul
Former Headmistress (Sr)
Faith Academy Delhi

* * *

Precious in the sight of the LORD, is the death of His saints.

Psalms 116:15

The pain and sorrow at the loss of loved ones to Covid-19 has left countless families confronting a sense of utter hopelessness. There is hardly anyone left untouched by the grief of loss. All across the world, the virus and death has left people mourning the loss of parents, children, husbands, wives, sons, daughters, brothers, sisters, friends, neighbors, colleagues, acquaintances etc.

In 2020, when Covid-19 struck in India, not many from the Christian community were affected and so many of us did not feel the pain. After all, our family, friends and loved ones were safe. Some of us felt some sympathy at the other lives being lost and the families traumatized. But, in April & May 2021, Covid-19 struck closer home and many of our family, friends and loved ones finished their earthly sojourn, leaving behind a trail of utter devastation, pain and tears. Some of the families are still unable to come out of the saddening experience.

But for us who love the Lord and believe in His Word, amidst these sorrowing and saddened moments, there is a sense of peace that flood our hearts and we experience comfort and consolation in the Presence and peace that Jesus gives. I saw first-hand the suffering and pain of my family members and colleagues during the 2nd wave of Covid-19. When we thought that it's over, we'd hear of another family or families being affected. Never did we realize that our loved ones would not return home from hospital.

When I heard of David bhaiya being also Covid positive, the first thought that came to my mind was, nothing will happen, he is a child of God and God will take care of him and bring him home. I was also aware that many of God's people-pastors, evangelists and men and women who loved the Lord had received their Home Call. There were concerted and sincere prayers for both David bhaiya and Alice bhabhi- for His healing touch. But it was not to be and God called David bhaiya to His eternal rest and Home. Left behind were the pain, sorrow and tears. The Funeral service brought a message of Hope and assurance because of Jesus' Resurrection.

Now, almost a year has gone by but the memories of a wonderful life-well lived before the Lord, lives on afresh in my memories. My earliest recollection of David bhaiya is that of a small boy, we would visit our Mamu-Mami's home in Allahabad and it was such a joy to enjoy the love and affection of the 5 elder brothers. David bhaiya always stood out as a bright and sharp student and everybody spoke highly of him. With the passage of time, David bhaiya pursued his studies and made a mark in his field of expertise as a Scientist. Our paths would cross once in a while and I always saw David bhaiya talk not of his job, post or position but his love for the Lord and how he is able to share Jesus in his workplace and with his colleagues. Because David bhaiya loved the Lord, the Lord had blessed him immensely in his profession as a Scientist and also blessed his dear family.

As I look back to my cousin's life, I thank God for using him as a witness for His namesake and also making his life a blessing for many. I would like to share some important traits in his life based on his name DAVID.

DEVOTED & DEDICATED TO GOD

AUTHENTIC PERSONALITY

VIBRANCY OF LIFE- HAPPY COUNTENANCE

INTEGRITY AT WORK- HONEST WITH STRONG MORAL VALUES & PRINCIPLES

DEVOTED & DEDICATED TO HIS FAMILY

David bhaiya's life was a life well lived for God and before people. He has gone ahead of us and we have a blessed assurance that one day we too will reach beyond the Golden shores to be with our Lord and meet our loved ones there.

TO GOD BE THE GLORY

Rev. Parvez Sethna
Allahabad

* * *

It is an honour for me to write a few lines about one of my childhood friend's and brother, David Samuel. We were brought up in homes that were very passionately related through friendship and Christian love. David 's mother whom we all lovingly called auntie Samuel was a very close friend of my mother. His four brothers and two of us when young made a team of noisy and naughty boys.

All of us grew up to be differently talented doing well in life and as families. David was especially closer to me because both of us were almost the same, age wise and also in our scientific temperament. I grew up to be a chemistry professor and David did well as a scientist. Even as adults we were close to each other as friends and both Alice and my wife gelled well as friends. His son Amit and my elder son studied together in the same engineering College. For me David was not only a friend and a brother but also someone with whom I discussed issues and questions in my spiritual journey. His untimely passing away due to Corona has shocked all of us in my family and many others in his church and the Prayag Raj community. The bond that we shared is unique and can't be expressed in words and sentences but I and VINITA with our sons Arpit and Shobhit and their families would want to assure Alice, Amit and Divya and their families that we won't be able to explain and express the loss we have suffered as individuals in the passing away of David.

At the same time the hope that we would meet again and enjoy the same love and fellowship in our eternal lives gives us hope and courage.

Dr. Lalit CT Eusebius

Retd. Vice- Principal and presently Burser, Ewing Christian College, Allahabad. 211003

Rev Dr. Vinita Eusebius

Principal, Girl's High School & College, Allahabad, 211001 & Ex. Associate Professor of Zoology, Ewing Christian College, Allahabad- 211003. Also presently Presbyter- in Charge, All Saints Cathedral, Allahabad- 211001.

* * *

Tribute to My Brother David Samuel
(by K. Vijayaragavan)

Let me start my tribute to dear brother David Samuel with the following prayer:

God, give us grace to accept with serenity
the things that cannot be changed,
Courage to change the things
which should be changed,
and the Wisdom to distinguish
the one from the other.

Living one day at a time,
Enjoying one moment at a time,
Accepting hardship as a pathway to peace,
Taking, as Jesus did,
This sinful world as it is,
Not as I would have it,
Trusting that You will make all things right,
If I surrender to Your will,
So that I may be reasonably happy in this life,
And supremely happy with You forever in the next.

Amen.

When I think of a verse that best describes the life of our beloved brother David Samuel, I am reminded of the following verse: "I have fought the good fight, I have finished the race, I have kept the faith. Finally, there is laid up for me the crown of righteousness, which the Lord, the righteous Judge, will give to me on that Day, and not to me only but also to all who have loved His appearing. (2 Timothy 4: 7-8).

"I have Kept the Faith"

I know Brother David Samuel for more than 40 years. It is David's faith in Jesus Christ that was the primary reason for my fellowship with him for such a long time. We both were part of different churches and had different spheres of work in God's kingdom, yet I was touched by his love for the Lord, love for the saints irrespective of denominational backgrounds. He was easily approachable, and his simplicity is noteworthy. From my association with David for a long period I could testify about his growth in his faith and fruits of the Spirit, and He kept His Faith till the end.

Brother David Samuel's motivation was rooted in his love for Christ: it shaped his integrity, his love of excellence in all spheres of life and his service for others.

"I have fought the Good Fight of Faith "

I have been one of the fellow companions of brother David in this earthly pilgrimage towards celestial city. I have shared his joys and sorrows. In all the struggle of this life, I have seen that he fought the good fight of faith.

Faith in Action

Brother David demonstrated his faith through good works. It is impossible for me to recount the number of times our paths have crossed during our lifetime. He was always there for me when I needed him and I was always there for him when he needed me.

I received his help, encouragements and advises in numerous ways. It is difficult to narrate all the incidents where we received the blessings of God through him. But one of the most common blessings was his help in securing admission in Faith Academy School for children of my friends. My last phone call was during his hospital stay in Pune, was regarding my request for his intervention to secure admission in Faith Academy which we cannot forget. May God bless his family and children.

Brother David has impacted so many lives through his life, example, training young brothers and sisters in truly fulfilling the last command of our Lord Jesus Christ.

"I have finished the race"

My last mobile conversation with brother David Samuel was during his hospitalisation due to covid in Pune. I was not knowing that was my final talk with him. But as I recall our conversation now, I could realise that he knew that he was going to finish his earthly race and enter into to the presence of the Lord. He has completed God's plan for his family, professional life, and in building the kingdom of God. He took pains in developing and maintaining Pusa Christian Fellowship.

Promises for Future

While death is always an intrusion to our earthly happiness and joy, its timing will not hinder us from our future hope.

Let us build our hope in the promises of our Lord Jesus Christ. "Let not your hearts be troubled. Believe in God. Believe also in me. I am the resurrection and the life. He who believes in me will live, even though he dies; and whoever lives and believes in me will never die. In this world you will have many trials and tribulations; but be of good cheer, for I have conquered the world."

Now I saw a new heaven and a new earth, for the first heaven and the first earth had passed away. Also, there was no more sea. Then I, John, saw the holy city, New Jerusalem, coming down out of heaven from God, prepared as a bride adorned for her husband. And I heard a loud voice from heaven saying, "Behold, the tabernacle of God *is* with men, and He will dwell with them, and they shall be His people. God Himself will be with them *and be* their God. And God will wipe away every tear from their eyes; there shall be no more death, nor sorrow, nor crying. There shall be no more pain, for the former things have passed away."

Then He who sat on the throne said, "Behold, I make all things new." And He said to me, "Write, for these words are true and faithful."

And He said to me, "It is done! I am the Alpha and the Omega, the Beginning and the End. I will give of the fountain of the water of life freely to him who thirsts (Revelation 21: 1-6).

No one will know the time of our death and the time of second coming of the Lord Jesus Christ. But for those who believe in the Lord, our absence from this earthly body is to be present with the Lord. One day we will meet, face to face our Maker and our Lord along with our beloved ones.

Dr. K. Vijayaragavan
Former Director, IARI, New Delhi

* * *

Thanks be to God for the life of brother David Samuel as he served the Lord wholeheartedly, worked in his office diligently and took care of his family lovingly. I remember brother as a very caring, loving and soft-spoken person. He used to recognize each person with his greetings and with radiant smile whenever he met them. He was a very hospitable and a very concerned person. I remember him as a very enthusiastic hard-working brother when he performed a role of a good father in one of my Christian short films. Now brother is enjoying the loving presence of our Lord in Heaven, leaving this message behind what apostle Paul said," I have fought the good fight, I have finished the race, I have kept the faith." 2 Timothy 4:7.

Sheila Samuel

* * *

यादें

डेविड विजय कुमार सेमुएल, जिन्हें हम सेमुएल साहब के नाम से बुलाते थे, एक बहुत ही नेकदिल, न्याय - प्रिय इंसान और कर्तव्यों के प्रति ईमानदार व्यक्तित्व के धनी थे। वे एक उच्च श्रेणी के अभियंता और वैज्ञानिक होने के साथ- साथ, मानवीय गुणों से परिपूर्ण, सामाजिक कर्तव्यों के प्रति जागरूक व्यक्ति थे। स्वाभाविक तौर पर धार्मिक और आध्यात्मिक प्रतिबद्धता से उनके स्वभाव में उच्चतर स्थिरता और बलवान नैतिकता थी।

हमारा उनसे परिचय सन 1973 में हुआ जब मैंने इलाहाबाद ऐग्रिकल्चरल इंस्टिट्यूट में ईंजीनियरिंग में दाखिल लिया। वे हमसे एक साल आगे थे। इलाहाबाद के ही होने के नाते वे अपने घर से कालेज आते - जाते थे। इलाहाबाद की पढ़ाई पूरी करने के बाद वे आईआईटी

खड़गपुर गए, जहाँ एक साल बाद मैं भी गया। वहाँ भी हमारा साथ बना रहा और यह साथ 1978 तक बना रहा। मेरी खुसकिस्मती थी कि हमने उसी प्रोजेक्ट पर काम किया और आगे बढ़ाया, जिसपर एक साल पहले सेमुएल साहब ने काम किया था। वहाँ के बाद नौकरी के लिए वे वैज्ञानिक चयनित होकर ICAR में गए और एक साल बाद मैंने राष्ट्रीय बीज निगम में कार्य शुरू किया। थोड़े समय के बाद हम दोनों ही अपने- अपने विभागों की तरफ से दिल्ली में आ गए। उनका अभियांत्रिकी विभाग और राष्ट्रीय बीज निगम में पास ही होने के नाते हम लोग फिर एक जगह हो गए। शुरू में हम दोनों ही दिल्ली में इंदरपुरी में रहते। एक जगह रहते हमारे बीच पारिवारिक घनिष्ठता बढ़ती गई।

एक समय आया जब हम दिल्ली में अपने लिए एक स्थायी निवास की खोज में निकले तो दोनों ने द्वारका में निवास बनाया। अपनी पारिवारिक जिम्मेदारियों के निर्वहन में वे पुणे रहने लगे थे और मैं भी द्वारका से नोयडा आ गया, लेकिन हमारी बातचीत और संपर्क बराबर बना रहा। हमारी नजदीकियाँ इतनी थीं कि एक दूसरे को काम केवल बता देने मात्र से होना सुनिश्चित हो जाता था। हमारे संबंधों में औपचारिकता का कोई स्थान नहीं था बल्कि एकात्मकता की अधिकता थी। पद भले बढ़ते गए हों, जिम्मेदारियाँ बढ़ती गई हो, लेकिन हमारे आपसी व्यवहार में कभी कोई अंतर आया ही नहीं। मुझे याद है कि एक बार हमारा एक साथी आकर मुझे सेमुएल साहब से सिफारिश करने को कहा ताकि उसके पोते का एडमिशन हो सके। मैंने उसे बताकर मिलने की सलाह दी और उसके काम हो गया।

मेरे लिए सेमुएल साहब आज भी अपने परिवार, अपने विचार, व्यवहार और आध्यात्मिक उत्कर्षता के नाते, उतनी ही सशक्तता के साथ, हमारे साथ हैं। आत्मा अमर है। वे जहां कहीं भी हों, उन्हें प्रभु अपना साथ और आशीर्वाद दें।

(अवधेश कुमार सिंह)

589, सेक्टर-19, पॉकेट-2, नई-दिल्ली

फोन: 9910491556

मेल: nscaks@gmail.com

* * *

My Memories with Dr. DVK Samuel

It gives me great pain while I write this memoir of my dear friend, philosopher and guide who left for his heavenly abode in the summer of 2021. Honestly, I don't remember when I first met Dr. Samuel. Must have got in touch with him through our common friend Dr. Debashish Nag in the late eighties. Our life in Pusa campus was simple yet peaceful, there was balanced harmony around us. We used to gather in the bus stop during early morning hours, and that was time for some informal chit chat. He was extremely friendly with an affectionate smile on his face and always exchanged warm pleasantries with people. It's difficult to believe that God will never give us an opportunity to enjoy such moments with him ever.

Though I was few years his junior, but we both were eventually posted in postharvest technology division of IARI, New Delhi. Hence, we shared many hours together discussing/solving various intricate researchable issues maintaining a perfect blend between process engineering and post-harvest horticulture. He was a very kind hearted and soft-spoken gentleman and I never saw him scolding anybody even when he was holding the position of professor and head in the Division of PHT at IARI. In government service one always faces personal ups and downs. When I was going through such a rough patch, he was the first person to give me moral support in his own capacity and positively encouraged me to overcome it. I rarely found him using his positional power in office, rather he used his personal charm to win the hearts of people around him. Christmas always brings back my best memories with Dr. Samuel and his family. He used to bake large batches of specially baked Christmas cakes.

Our children loved the sumptuous spread offered at his house on 25th December. Those happy evenings are etched permanently in our mind. May God rest his soul in peace.

Prof. (Dr) Ram Krishna Pal
Former Director, ICAR-NRCP, Solapur, Maharashtra &
Ex-Prof. & Head, Div of PHT, ICAR-IARI, New Delhi

* * *

I remember late Dr. DVK Samuel as a great soul, a wonderful teacher, dedicated researcher, lovely friend, and guide. He symbolized as a fountain of love, stream of kindness, ever ready to help. He is liked and loved by his students, colleagues, seniors, and teachers for dedication, commitment, punctuality, and above all clear and pious heartedness. A large number of employees of IARI are indebted to him and his wife Mrs. Alice for the primary school education of their wards. Even after superannuation he continued to help and guide ICAR, IARI staff and others. In this regard, Dr. Samuel was famous for selflessness and forgiveness; two very important characteristics of a noble soul. During his tenure as Head of Division, I served as Professor (In charge Academics) of the Division and received all love, care and guidance. His out of box thinking, foresightedness and meticulous approach was par excellence. I very emotionally recall the discussion with him on 29th April, 2015; he was about to retire on 30th April and I got office order for Divisional Head on 28th evening; I requested him to continue till 30th and retire as Head of Division but he said "no', you join on 29th; it is important for you; it does not matter for me". This was the greatness of late Dr. Samuel, his selflessness. I salute the noble soul and pray for best wishes to his family.

With Regards

Indra Mani
Head, Agril. Engg, IARI

* * *

Eulogium in Honour of the Late Dr. DVK Samuel

Dr. DVK Samuel was a very good family friend of ours. God enabled us to meet with this wonderful family and to have a close fellowship with them for about 20 years. He was very regular in coming to Church and every Sunday we used to meet him after the service and he always came forward to greet people with a welcoming smile on his face and chat for a while. Dr. Samuel was a gentle, soft spoken, humble and helpful person which made him more approachable for people to freely interact with him. Besides this, we used to meet him as EGF (Evangelical Graduate Fellowship) family and enjoyed a very good fellowship at his residence in PUSA, as his home was an open home for many students' ministry. The way he was involved in conducting God's ministry, his family and his work, is an example to follow. His care and concern for his acquaintances were always genuine and sincere. We certainly miss his personal touch which we enjoyed with him as a family and we are sure that his untimely calling to the Heavenly Home would be an irreparable void to all the dear and near ones. Our prayers are with Alice, Amit & family and Divya & family.

Mr. and Mrs. Titus

* * *

I have fought the good fight, I have finished the race, I have kept the faith.
2 Timothy 4:7

It was in 1979-80 that I came in contact with Dr. DVK Samuel when he joined Agriculture Research Service (ARS) of ICAR. We were together for the rural training program at Vaishali (Bihar). Two more ARS trainee scientists, Dr. R.D.Singh and Dr. A.S.Baba joined us and we were staying in the Circuit House of Vaishali. I remember Dr. Samuel for his great enthusiasm, outgoing personality, and sense of humour which made our stay in that lonely village very pleasant and memorable. His drive, energy and desire to excel made him one of the best scientists in the country in the field of post-harvest technology and process engineering. In recognition of his excellent contributions to agriculture and industry, he was appointed as Head, Division of Agricultural Engineering, IARI, New Delhi. Later on, he was also selected as Adjunct Professor in the College of Agricultural Engineering, Dr. Rajendra Prasad Central Agricultural University, PUSA (Bihar) for the period 2018-19 where he helped in developing research projects, providing guidance to scientists and teaching of courses to PG students of the university. Dr. Samuel was also a member of Research Advisory Committee (RAC) of ICAR-Central Citrus Research Institute, Nagpur for a period of 3 years, beginning 2018 till 2020.

Dr. Samuel was one of the foremost Indian researchers in Process Engineering with more than 50 publications in reputed national and international journals. On the professional front, he will be remembered for various innovations like solar-powered vending cart & evaporative cooling system for storage of fruits and vegetables, manually operated tomato harvesting tool for greenhouse, modelling of tomato seedling growth in greenhouse, and many such initiatives directly benefitting the farmers. Dr. Samuel was a cardinal figure in process engineering and his colleagues and students loved him. For many, he was a friend, mentor and guide. As a faithful servant of Lord Jesus Christ, Dr. Samuel has left an indelible mark on the hearts and minds of people who have worked with him in IARI and other places. His youthful spirit, full of wisdom, kindness and an uncanny sense of dignity, shall continue to stimulate and guide us forever.

Undoubtedly, the untimely demise of Dr. Samuel is a big loss not only to the fraternity of Agricultural Engineers in India, but also to the farming community. As we struggle to accept the irreparable loss of our colleague, we remain ever grateful for his tremendous contributions to the country and the joy and cheers he brought to his family, friends, colleagues and students.

My sincere prayers to the Almighty that the noble soul rests in eternal peace.

Dr. S. Solomon

Ex-Vice-Chancellor: CSA University of Agri. & Technology, Kanpur, India
Ex-Director: Indian Institute of Sugar Cane Research, Lucknow-India:
Editor-in-Chief: Sugar Tech Journal (Springer Nature)

* * *

In Fond Remembrance of Late Dr. DVK Samuel

It must have been in early 1980s that I have known Dr. DVK Samuel who was working as Scientist in the Division of Agricultural Engineering at IARI, New Delhi. I too had joined IARI in August 1978 like him. We soon became buddies. Luckily, we became neighbours too in the campus. It was our good fortune. And this involved "must visit" greeting each other on the occasion of Christmas and Diwali for both families, besides other get-togethers. It was a pleasure to talk to him and his family. He was always in a jovial mood. Occasionally, we talked about our interests in agricultural research, education and extension. He would explain the farm technologies that he and his colleagues were developing. And the simplicity with which he explained the importance and working of his farm machineries impressed me a lot. A specialist in post-harvest farm machinery, Dr. Samuel understood the importance of solar energy early enough to be in forefront, and developed solar powered machineries like dehydrator for onion, screen cleaner for seeds, solar cooled vegetable cart for farmers, etc. He has three patents to his credit. Over the years, he achieved an academic excellence that we all admired. As a Head of Division of Agricultural Engineering at IARI, Dr. Samuel steered the course of research and development of farm equipments and implements to make them more purposeful, efficient and economical to the needs of farm community. He was also a guide and teacher that the students loved. He earned the IARI best teacher award in 2006. He published more than 60 research papers which are well cited. He received awards and recognitions from Institution of Engineers (India) and Indian Society of Agricultural Engineers on more than one occasions. We remained in contact even after our retirement and so were our families. So, I owe him and his family our knowledge of great learning of Christian faith and culture. It is great to see that he and his wife Alice raised their children Divya and Amit in the best Christian faith and values, and are very nice friends of ours and our children, carrying a legacy of being good humane in the society. Even after retirement, Dr. Samuel involved himself actively in agricultural education and research and community service. So the news of his death last year was a sad setback to all his family, relatives and friends. For us, it is also a loss of our renowned farm scientist which is difficult to forget. But life must go on, as "God is our merciful Father and the source of all comfort. He comforts us in all our troubles so that we can comfort others" (2 Corinthians 1:4). Amen.

Govind & Nalini Gujar
New Delhi

* * *

Dr. DVK Samuel

The very mention of his name brings to memory endless images and description of Agricultural produce, its health benefits and remedial capability each may have. One always saw agricultural science in the form of David Samuel.

David was passionate about science of agriculture but His passion for the Lord Jesus and His Word was even more evident and this priority was always clear. He lived a life that portrayed the compassion and integrity of the Saviour He loved and served.

Yetoly and I got to know David closely over last 6 years. 'Tea party' every morning was highlight of each day. There was never a dull moment with David around. He was always fun to be with. He invested his life in others and has a legacy we can be proud of where he built lives during his life tenure here.

Shakti Verma
New Delhi

* * *

Dr. DVK Samuel - A Great Character

Dr. DVK Samuel has been a person of immense value and a great character. I have long and cherished memories of Dr. Samuel. It dates back to our college days at Allahabad Agricultural Institute (now known as SHUATS), Allahabad. After a couple of years of break, as we were from different batches, this association was again actively revived when he joined Indian Agricultural Research Institute, New Delhi. As both of us were from Allahabad, many a times among other things we would fondly remember our college days; its canteen and the delicious *Sweets* and *Namkeens* from famous shops of the city. He would always welcome everyone with a smiling face. Who can forget his New Year Parties with delicious cakes?

Dr. Samuel is well known for his professional achievements; awards and recognitions. It was my privilege to write a book entitled "Mechanization of vegetable production and post-harvest management" with Dr. Samuel as one of the authors. The book not only earned recognitions but also won best book award of Indian Society of Agricultural Engineers (ISAE). My last meeting with Dr. Samuel was in a meeting at Indian Agricultural Research Institute, New Delhi when he told me that he has partially settled at Pune. Then came the unexpected shock news of his departure to the heavenly abode. May his soul rest in peace.

Wherever you are Dr. Samuel, we will always remember you.

Dr. A. P. Srivastava

* * *

As I sit down to write about David bhaiya as I used to call him, my thoughts go back to when we were called first cousins but as I grew up, we came to know that we had no blood relation but in spite of that, all the siblings of the family were connected to each other with love and affection. He was the best brother from amongst the five brothers, very loving and affectionate. After marriage when he met my husband, they both bonded very well and even went to South Korea together and their bond kept growing with time. After my husband went to be with the Lord, bhaiya was concerned for me and my kids. Then he introduced me to Faith Academy family where he constantly showed his concern about my welfare. His sudden death was extremely shocking I just could not believe it as just four days back I had wished him birthday greeting. It was unbelievable that he was gone but is now in a better place with his Creator. David bhaiya was a very soft hearted, affectionate and considerate brother. I will always be grateful to you for all that you were to me and my family. Love you bhaiya!

Mrs. Parveen Nath
Delhi

* * *

He had a heart that cared completely. His smile brought immense pleasure. His love brought joy beyond measure. These words fit truly when we talk about Dr. DVK Samuel lovingly called "Bhaiya"by me. Being a Senior scientist, Chairperson/ Member of the Management Committee of Faith Academy and other renowned Committees all over India, he never was a proud person, rather was a living example of humbleness and simplicity. Bhaiya used to enjoy every bit of his life to the fullest. He was a food lover and used to appreciate the hospitality rendered to him at all times. A true man of God who had honoured God through his life at all times. He was a thoughtful and generous person, who was devoted completely towards his work and family. He had embodied all the positive qualities in his children and grandchildren that he himself possessed. He was a loving and committed husband, whose memories will forever be cherished by his wife.

"Well done, good and faithful servant. You have been faithful over
a little;
I will set you over much. Enter into the joy of your master".

Matthew 25:21

With warm thoughts and care, blessings and prayers:

Neeta Mall

(Headmistress-Middle School, Faith Academy)

* * *

DVK Samuel is not just a name. He was an inspiration for us. He was a
wonderful husband, father and my loving uncle (chacha). He was very
hardworking and never left learning and teaching. He was a very good
guide. For me he was a father like figure. Chacha if you can hear I want to
tell you that I love you and miss you a lot.

Sheeba (David's niece)

* * *

प्रो॰ मान सिंह
परियोजना निदेशक
Prof. Man Singh
Project Director

जल प्रौद्योगिकी केन्द्र

भा० कृ० अ० प० – भारतीय कृषि अनुसंधान संस्थान
नई दिल्ली–110012
WATER TECHNOLOGY CENTRE
ICAR-INDIAN AGRICULTURAL RESEARCH INSTITUTE
NEW DELHI-110012

दिनांकः 05 मार्च, 2022

संदेश

डॉ. डी.वी.के. सैमुअल से हमारा पारिवारिक गहरा रिश्ता पिछले 35 वर्षों से रहा। उनका अचानक हम लोगों को छोड़कर परलोक जाना असमायिक रहा। डॉ. सैमुअल बहुत ही सरल स्वभाव के थे। हमेशा सहज रहते थे। जब वे कृषि अभियांत्रिकी संभाग के अध्यक्ष थे, उन दिनों हम लोगों का उनसे बार–बार विचार विमर्श होता था। बैठकों में मिलते थे। हमेशा प्रसन्नचित रहते थे। हम लोग एक दूसरे के परिवार के सकुशलता के बारे में भी अक्सर पूछ–ताछ तथा शुभकामनाओं का आदान प्रदान कर लिया करते थे। डॉ. सैमुअल एवं श्रीमती सैमुअल फेथ एकेड्मी में बहुत सक्रिय होते थे। उसके कारण पूसा संस्थान के बच्चों को सैमुअल दंपति का स्नेह और आशीर्वाद मिलता था। उनकी ही कृपा से अनेकों बच्चों को फेथ एकेड्मी में गुणवत्ता पूर्ण प्रारम्भिक और माध्यामिक शिक्षा प्राप्त करने का सुअवसर मिला। मेरा परिवार सदैव डॉ. सैमुअल जैसी पुण्य आत्मा का सदा आभारी रहेगा। आपके साथ बिताए हुए लम्बे समय की ढेरों मधुर यादें सदा मन और चित्त में बसी रहेंगी। डॉ. सैमुअल परिवार के प्रति मेरी संवेदनाएँ और शुभकामनाएँ सत्त साथ रहेंगी।

सादर,

मान सिंह

Tel: 011-25846790   Mob : 9899322664 Email: pd_wtc@iari.res.in

Memoir of DVK Samuel

Dr. DVK Samuel, my co-brother, fondly called DVK by all the family members was an amazing family man with a family-work life balance. He spent quality time with his wife and children and created a unique DNA for his family with distinct values. Having a flair for exploring new places and for travelling, his outings and family vacations together were woven into their family culture meticulously.

Their extended family was huge with four of his siblings and seven of his wife Alice's, my wife Shanti being one of them. They took lot of efforts to build in strong bonding with all of the loved ones and families and rose up to any situation needing their love, care and help.

They were so social to cultivate friendship with many, and nurtured a wide array of mutually blessed relationships leaving behind a trail of them wherever they went. They were known for their love and hospitality as they hosted many families and young people, cared for them, prayed, counselled and established them.

Their hearts were moved towards those who are needy around them and took steps to practically alleviate their sufferings. He together with his wife Alice became philanthropists were part of many NGOs the chief among them being Pandita Ramabai Mukti Mission for the Destitute women at Pune and Hope Care Trust, Caring for Children in Crisis at Hubli. They imparted the same values to their children Amit Mark and Divya so much so that now Amit and his mother Alice continue their family culture by being some of the main supporters of Hope Care Trust and Divya who continually supports various NGO's like CEF and Sahayak to name a few.

With relatives at Hubli

Dr. DVK Samuel with his visionary foresight and administrative skills which God has bestowed upon him was in the Board of Faith Academy School facilitating it to grow and become an exemplary school in Delhi. This was in addition to many other Christian NGOs like Haggai Institute, Delhi Bible Fellowship, Child Evangelical Fellowship and Seva Bharat that he served.

Being a Scientist and intelligent thinker, he stood tall among many of his peers in the field of Agricultural Engineering in Indian Agricultural Research Institute, Pusa, New Delhi. He carried his flair for research well beyond his time of retirement by his association with many other reputed institutes.

As he has gone to be with his Creator, his memories linger on and the legacy that he has passed on to his wife Alice Samuel, his son Amit Mark Samuel with Dr. Renate Samuel and their children Kartavya and Kaelyn and his daughter Divya Jairaj with Lalit Jairaj and their daughter Naina lives on through them. It's our prayer that God would bless this family to be a blessing to many.

Pastor R. Senthiappan
New life fellowship- Hubli

* * *

No words can explain the deep sorrow on the loss of our dear friend and brother DVK. Our relationship began over 30 years ago when we met at DBF church, where we all became one big family, there was David and Alice, Pastor Junias and Beth, JP and Nimmi, James and Hilda, Job and Jasmine, Mathai and Pat, Anup and Daisy, Ravi and Jharna, Paul Raj and Vaneja. We were all together here in Delhi and cherish the memories of those wonderful days, then life took us all in different directions yet we continued to stay connected. We would all get together for a meal and David would make his famous Shaami Kababs and Alice her Biriyani, we are going to miss that combination. We would have these long chats about life and what we would do after retirement, trips we needed to take but God had a different plan when he called David home so soon. We know that we will meet again, until then we will always have David's memory in our hearts.

Miss you my dear friend,

Deepak and Pam

* * *

With Friends from Delhi Bible Fellowship

Eulogy for Dr. DVK Samuel

I count it as a privilege to write few lines about the great & humble servant of God, who was called Home to be with His Saviour.

Dr. DVK Samuel, I have known him as a loving brother, who loved the Lord with all his heart, loved his family and was very passionate about his work at Pusa Institute, as well as the Chairman of the School Managing Committee of Faith Academy. He was a straight forward man and minced no words to express his thoughts and opinion, be it on any platform. I have a very special regard for him, as he was the man who was asked by the Search Committee of Grace Academy to give a report about me and my work in Allahabad (since he had a lot of contacts in Allahabad), while I was being considered as one of the prospective candidates for the post of the Principal at Grace Academy.

He was a very humble man and was very dignified in His ways. He was a man full of fun and laughter.

We thank God for the Saints like Dr. DVK Samuel and pray that what he has done for the Lord and His Kingdom will continue to yield fruits for God's glory.

With love & respect,

Benjamin Newton
Principal
Grace Academy

* * *

Dr. DVK Samuel was a man of great knowledge yet humble. He was greatly respected and loved at his workplace and church alike. He was a great encourager and always had a positive attitude towards life. He was a man of integrity and stood for discipline and biblical values.

I first remember meeting him at Delhi bible fellowship along with my family. He was known to my husband and my brother-in-law really well.

We as a family interacted and shared fine moments together promising to uphold each other's family in prayer.

He has left behind a legacy and some good memories that will be cherished by everyone who knew him.

His life reminds me of this verse from scripture, 2 Timothy 4:7 - "I have fought the good fight, I have finished the race, I have kept the faith."

Stella Das

* * *

With Parents and Relatives at Allahabad

My dearest brother, my own blood, Dr. David Samuel was a God fearing person. Very loving, affectionate at all times and helpful too. He had a great concern for his brothers and their families and would often visit us with great interest.

He was a very learned and an intellectual person. His steadfast love for all his brothers and their families can never be forgotten. In our time of trouble David gave us valuable advise and financial help too. He was a farsighted person and did his best for all of us. He had a great love for all nine children of our brothers and always found out about their well-being and progress in academics or career.

David feared God and often took me to his Church in Delhi. My brother David and my sister-in-law both had a great love and concern for us. I do pray for my sister- in-law Alice and her children, Amit and family and Divya and family that God may bless and keep them safe and healthy. Though I have a lot to say but I end here to say that he is loved and missed by us.

Rev Rajan Samuel
DVK's brother
Lucknow

* * *

Dr. Samuel was such an amazing, loving, caring, honest, good and honourable man of God. I can never forget how God put him in our lives. For me specially, Dr. Samuel was just like my own dad. When I became a Christian and I had to go through so much persecution Dr. Samuel and Alice ma'am stood with me. Even when I wanted to get married, I had no other support other than Dr. Samuel helping us so much. I would have never been able to come out of all the challenges and trauma I had gone through if it wasn't for Dr. Samuel who stood by me and my husband Stephen, and helped us to get married. God appointed Dr. Samuel to be there for us. And I am so grateful to God for his commitment to God and for his life. He was an encouraging guide and godly person. Even his birthday is the same date like my dad's, April 20th.My dad passed away in Jan 2011 but I still knew that Dr. Samuel and Alice ma'am were there for us. And I cannot forget all the Bible studies in their home and all the visits they would make to my home in Patel Nagar. My mom Kamal is in new Delhi but she still remembers all that Dr. Samuel and Alice ma'am have done for us. And I can never forget even after I got married to my husband Stephen and moved to Gurgaon, Dr. Samuel surprised us right after our wedding with some couples from the church who brought us so many gifts to start our life like fridge, utensils, bedsheets, food, money everything. You name it, we never forget that and we told about this to everyone in Canada as our testimony of God's faithfulness. Dr. Samuel was the one who inspired lives and generosity. And I even got ready for my wedding day in their place. Anna and Divya were my bridesmaids and Dr. Samuel and Alice Ma'am opened their home for me. Who does that so sacrificially? Only people who really love Jesus. And that is Dr. Samuel and Alice ma'am. I am forever grateful and touched by these precious people. And our regards and condolences are with Mrs. Samuel and her extended family. Dr. Samuel is in the best place in heaven with Jesus. No other place is better than that. I want to thank Dr. Samuel and Alice ma'am for all that they have done for us. Otherwise without their support and prayers we would not have made it. So, thanks so much and may the Lord bless you and keep you and your children and grandchildren and your generations to come Be blessed and May the Lord make His face shine on you all.

Kind Regards and Thanks,

Poonam and Stephen and children

* * *

My brother-in-law late Dr. DVK Samuel was a very God fearing, humble and generous person. When my younger sister Tabitha who had cancer came to India, before she died. All brothers and sisters with our spouses and children stayed at his place. (We are 8 siblings in our family). You can imagine the big crowd. Both David and Alice took good care of us. On different occasions likewise we would gather at his place. He was cordial with all age groups. Even children also enjoyed talking to him. He also took part in the advisory board of some Christian Organizations.

At this juncture, I wish Alice, Amit and Divya along with their families the peace of God which passes all understanding, and a Christ centred life ahead.

Rathna
(Alice's sister) and Emmanuel Amarnath- Delhi

* * *

I know Dr. Samuel from the days of IIT Kharagpur. He had a very pleasant personality and every body wanted to be friends with him. He was one of the well dressed, well mannered and soft spoken person. He was one year senior to me at IIT Kharagpur but was always like a friend to us. Later on we both joined Agricultural Research Service as scientists. Dr. Samuel had headed two important departments namely Post Harvest Technology and Agricultural Engineering division of the prestigious Indian Agricultural Research Institute at Delhi. He has worked on many innovative projects in food engineering, guided and mentored many students for masters and PhD. The sudden demise of Dr. Samuel has shocked all of us. He will be forever remembered for his contributions to the profession of agricultural engineering in general and food process engineering in particular. I pray to the Almighty for eternal peace to the departed soul and give strength to the family members to bear his loss.

Dr. R T Patil

Former Director, ICAR-Central Institute of Post Harvest
Engineering and Technology, Ludhiana, Punjab

* * *

It gives me great pleasure to share my experience regarding my time spent with Dr. Samuel, the simplest and nicest man in my life who helped me a lot professionally. He was a very competent man who not only served in the premier institute of India for many many years but also headed a very big Engineering Division, he was one of the top most Agricultural Engineers of India and developed innovative technologies which not only supported the science but also helped the Indian farmers to reduce cost of cultivation by adopting Mechanisation.

He was also associated with educational institutions to promote education among the poor masses. I closely came in contact with Dr. Samuel in 2006 when I joined as the Director of Maize Research (DMR) IARI, Pusa campus.

I found Dr. Samuel very supportive, positive, cooperative and always ready to help those who approached him. He was so simple in his life and accessible to anybody and above all a great human being.

His untimely departure to heaven is a great loss to the field of science, the social society, friends and above all to the family as whole. To me his permanent absence is a great loss.

I wish and pray to the Almighty that it is well with his soul.

Dr. Sain Dass
Ex Director Maize

* * *

Dr. David Vijay Kumar Samuel: The departure of a great soul is of great loss to me in particular. I have got the opportunity to meet, discuss and interact with Dr. Samuel several times. I was introduced to David by Dr. S P Agrawala. I went to NDRI several times to appear before him. He was the friend among the friends. Later on, I was greatly comforted by his father-in-law, Shri Prasad during my stay at Kharagpur. Prasad Sir came to my flat in ZH Hall several times just to comfort us. He suggested a religious gentleman to PRAY for my recovery from Asthma. I also interacted with Dr. David in IARI in times of his Headship of the Divisions in Post Harvest Technology and Agricultural Engineering. I am still searching a friend and well-wisher as good as Dr. Samuel. One desirable quality is rare these days. David almost never criticized his colleagues in their absence. He rather used the title 'sahib' for almost all seniors in their absence. I went to participate in his marriage at Faridabad. He was faithful to his friends. I heard almost no ill of David from anybody. This is my real memory.

May his soul rest in peace. Thanks.

Dr. Bhawani Shanker Modi
(Scientist)
Karnal, Haryana.

* * *

David Vijay Kumar Samuel for many but for me he was "Sam". It was sometime in September, 1971 when my father introduced me to one of his colleagues Sri. Robert Samuel. After pleasantry, Robert Samuel Uncle told me that his son is in final year of Intermediate and most probably will be joining Agricultural Engineering course. Next year in 1972 uncle called me and introduced a shy boy and told that he is joining the course and being a senior, I should take care of him. That was the start of my friendship with "Sam" which continued for next 49 years. He followed me at IIT, Kharagpur for MTech and later we both submitted our thesis in 1978. I had delayed my thesis submission due to joining of job. Later we both qualified Agriculture Research Service (ARS) in 1978 and what a coincidence, we both joined at Vivekananda Parvatiya Krishi Anusandhan Sansthan, Almora with a gap of 4 days. Now, we were colleagues, both were bachelors and we spent our evenings together. Those were early days and as a scientist, we were not very clear how to proceed but under the sharp eyes of our Director, Dr. J.P. Tandon, we both progressed. However, he shifted to NDRI, Karnal within a year, while I continued at Almora for the next 16 years. We both continued to grow in our respected fields and again we got together at IIT, Kharagpur for Ph.D. and we both completed our Doctoral with a difference of one year. He continued at IARI, New Delhi and rose to Head of Division there. I shifted to Bhubaneswar and later to Port Blair as Director, but we were always in touch with each other, shared our joys of success and moments of despair. It was a rare bond of friendship, which was not affected by our status and by our achievements in service. We always felt happy with each other's success and supported each other. I remember in summer of 2006, when I had to go to see a boy for my daughter, he accompanied me to Gurgaon and we both interviewed the man, who later became my Son-in-law. We would recollect those moments and laughed about it whenever we met. Again in 2009, it was a time of joy when his daughter Divya got married at Delhi. I along with my wife flew from Portblair to Delhi to attend the marriage of his daughter. Thus, we shared our achievements in my personal lives too. He retired in 2015 from ICAR services but continued to be active in professional work. When I joined as Vice-Chancellor at Pusa, Bihar, he was always available on call to help me in selection of different committees whenever required.

Never thought that he will leave us so early. He still had many years to contribute to the profession and I was looking forward for involving him in university activities. He had already served as adjunct Professor in our College of Agricultural Engineering, Pusa (Bihar) and was a favorite teacher among students. But God has some other plan. This Covid took him from us. While writing these lines for him, I can just say Sam I miss you, I miss your laughter and I miss your support. You are with God. I pray Almighty to give you eternal peace. With love and affection.

Yours,

R.C.
(The name by which he used to call me)
Vice Chancellor, Pusa, Bihar

* * *

Professor Dr. Vijay Kumar Samuel was my student in M.Tech in the course Crop Process Engineering at IIT Kharagpur. He was very well behaved and studious student, very friendly with his classmates and teachers. While at IIT-KGP, Samuel showed very mature and intelligent behaviour. He was friendly with his classmates and we very fondly remember him.

In his professional career at the Indian Agricultural Research Institute he excelled to become professor and head of the department of Agricultural Engineering and occupied prestigious posts in the Indian Society of Agricultural Engineering. I have a lot of respect for his work and deeds. Wish him peace in the other world.

Satish Bal
Professor-IIT kharagpur

* * *

David and I met for the first time at Hyderabad during ARS training. Since he was alone from his institute, he joined our group of ARS probationers from Delhi. I remember him as a very jovial, supportive and helpful man. Later he was transferred to NDRI karnal (my home town). He was very social with my parents and my siblings. Good men are always taken away early by God. He will always remain in our hearts. May God provide peace to his soul.

Kumkum Walia
(colleague of Dr. DVK Samuel)

* * *

It was the second wave of Covid, the deadliest one in India, we all were scared and helpless. The monster was indiscriminately picking up our near and dear ones from all of us. In those tense moments, I learnt the news of the sad demise of my dear friend Sam. It had shaken me to the core. I was pushed back by four and a half decades to Kharagpur, where I first met Sam my friend for life, a gentle and ever smiling young man. We had shared experience in office and with family for over four decades. I had such a wonderful interpersonal relationship with him that we could discuss our every problem whether in office or in family without any hitch.

I always appreciated his clarity in vision in dealing with issues in hand. He always remained firmly grounded and arrived at the right decision in these circumstances. The precautionary admission of Divya (daughter) in Mt Carmel School, though being in Management of Faith Academy was an illustration he again demonstrated his precautionary approach in ensuring admission of Divya in Commerce, her dream subject.

For over three decades as colleagues, we never had any fight or any tangible disagreement. We could laugh at official issues and remained good friends in office also.

I did enjoy his unrestricted support in all my endeavours without asking. I have lost him in this physical world but he continues to live with me forever.

J.K. Singh
Scientist IARI, New Delhi

* * *

D.V.K.SAMUEL THE WAY LIVED WELL

(Eulogy By Paulraj)

When are we going to watch your smile dear Sam DVK?

Men and women we all recall your legacy that won't decay.

Though it looks like you're now gone so far away,

We know you are with Christ watching us every day!

Books you wrote with research on land and environment in our hand

Are going to enrich scientists on plants with facts to understand.

Future of the world for sure will benefit from topics you planned

 For people and pupil in every chapter with facts you command.

We all tend to forget the departed through passing years,

They all say so, but being close to you for years,

When we see things you used and hear your voice through ears

Playing your audios videos , we just burst into tears!

Lord, as we think of life on earth through life of Samuel our dear,

We now know importance of life after death we draw near

Help us talk to you for anything and everything from you to hear

What you want us to know to live eternally with you and cheer!

We live here in this world believing we are not alone

Hoping you always with us till we reach our permanent home!

My Best Half

Where do I begin?… My mind is clouded with so many thoughts. Firstly, I want to say that I am so blessed and fortunate to have had him as my husband. I thank God for him.

He was a wise and intelligent man, from receiving gold medals to getting the best teacher's award, writing papers, writing books on his subject, fabricating machines for various agricultural purposes and being a guide to a number of PhD students. He was not one who burnt the midnight oil. Once home he was for us. Yes, to go through PhD thesis, he would do it in a systematic way by dividing his work into smaller tasks completing some portion of it every day and thus finish the entire thesis. Each student's thesis has been kept safely with me now, including my husband's. He was very cool, never in panic. He achieved all this during his working hours. He was very systematic and organized in his work.

He was a perfectionist with a human touch, a complete family man. During winters he would tuck the children in bed with a hot water bottle to keep their feet warm or he would tell them stories and put them to sleep while I cleared the kitchen and got things ready for the next day. He was always there to lend a helping hand. When cooking he would come forward to give me a glass of cold water, or help me in chopping vegetables, spreading the table and even drying the clothes. He encouraged me in my hobbies like gardening, trying out new recipes and keeping an aquarium.

We had division of labour at home, I was responsible in disciplining the children and getting them to study. He was always on the same page with me in this regard.

I have never travelled alone except for two over sea trips and once to Pune. I have never seen him cry, always cheerful and enjoyed life. He loved get-togethers and travelling. He has shown me almost the whole of India. Our foreign trips were even more enjoyable going with our group of people, enjoying different foods, sightseeing and of course going out shopping.

He daily remembered every grandchild in his prayers. Naina when small would watch TV with him and would go to sleep on his shoulder. Kaelyn being the youngest felt like a princess with him. Kartavya the gentle boy was the Apple of his eye. He enjoyed spending time with them and they looked forward for their birthday gifts. I never had the opportunity to complain that he forgot my birthday, he remembered every one of our birthdays even my siblings. In the month of March 2021, I told him we will celebrate our 40th Wedding Anniversary on June 16 he said ''No we will celebrate our 50th wedding Anniversary." God has His own plans…

Till the end I thought he would make it. I grieve his loss.

"I miss you David and look forward to meeting you in heaven. I thank God for the wonderful life we spent together and for the years we spent with our children and grandchildren that God has given us. You are loved and remembered each day by all of us."

* * *

Together in Switzerland

Enjoying Vacation

Memories Don't Fade...
they Will Always Remain with Us...

Alice